FIFE
THE MINING KINGDOM

A haulage road at Michael Colliery, 1930.

Guthrie Hutton

Stenlake Publishing
1999

SCOTLAND'S
BLACK DIAMONDS
SCOTTISH MINING MUSEUM

This book has been produced in association with
the Scottish Mining Museum, Lady Victoria Colliery, Newtongrange.

First Published in the United Kingdom, 1999
by Stenlake Publishing, Ochiltree Sawmill,
The Lade, Ochiltree, Ayrshire, KA18 2NX
Telephone / Fax: 01290 423114

ISBN 1 84033 092 9

A picking table at Cowdenbeath.

A female 'putter' in 1842.

INTRODUCTION

It is likely that coal was being used in Fife long before the first recorded instance in 1291, when the Abbot of Dunfermline was given authority to work outcrops of coal in Pittencrieff Glen. Coal is often found exposed in the sides of valleys and glens, and sometimes on the surface, pushed upwards by geological forces. The first miners hacked into these outcrops, initially to provide domestic fuel, but later for industrial use too.

The first major coal-using industry in Fife was salt evaporation. Boiling sea water to make salt may sound like a quaint old custom, but it was in fact a huge industry and a vital part of the Scottish economy. It flourished on both sides of the Forth estuary where coal was found close to the sea. The water was boiled in large, rectangular iron salt pans which were set up in special pan houses at various places around the coast. Initially they were run by the monasteries that controlled much of Scotland's land and wealth, but after the Reformation of 1560 they came under the control of big landowners who sought to work them for profit. This created an unstable labour market which the Scottish Parliament attempted to regularise by passing a law in 1606 that bound miners and salters to their place of work – in effect making slaves of them. The law was repealed in 1799. The laird of Fordell freed his miners a year earlier and for years afterwards people celebrated with a parade – the Fordell Paraud.

A 'Fifeshire Putter' from the 1842 Children's Employment Commission Report.

Although they were free, the miners continued to work in dreadful conditions, with women and children alongside them. In 1842 the Children's Employment Commission was set up by Parliament to investigate. The commissioners found that industrialisation in the west of Scotland had forced changes, but that mining conditions in Fife and the Lothians were still amongst the worst in Britain. Parliament was so shocked by the Commission's report that it banned women and girls, and boys under ten, from underground work.

Fife's mines remained relatively small. Most of what was mined was exported from small harbours like Charlestown, St David's and West Wemyss. Iron working was developed at Oakley and Lochgelly, but it did not match the huge industries of the west, and so never provided the conditions for growth. Then, in the last quarter of the nineteenth century, mining in Fife suddenly became a major industry, a development that coincided with the rapid expansion of rail and sea transport. Both needed coal – and Fife coal was ideal – but as well as burning it themselves, steam ships and locomotives carried coal to markets at home and abroad.

The world wanted Fife's coal and ports at Methil and Burntisland were developed to export it. Output leapt and millions of tons were poured into the holds of ships bound for customers from Scandinavia to South America. Local companies and interlopers from Lanarkshire developed mines, but the industry came to be dominated by three major concerns: the Fife Coal Company, the Lochgelly Iron and Coal Company, and the Wemyss Coal Company.

Tipping on the Nellie bing with Glencraig behind.

The First World War brought the seemingly unstoppable rise in exports to a halt and they never fully recovered. The coal companies struggled to re-establish markets throughout the troubled 1920s and 1930s and then, as prospects began to improve, they had to cope with another world war. When it was over, the industry was nationalised. At the time, the Fife Coal Company was Scotland's largest coal company controlling half the industry in Fife. It worked the country's most modern pit, Comrie, while its great rival, the Wemyss Coal Company, operated the two largest pits, Michael and Wellesley. Now a major mining area, Fife was about to become even more important.

'Vesting Day' for the new National Coal Board was 1st January 1947. New capacity was urgently needed to meet the demands of a nation trying to rebuild after the war and the NCB sank two huge super-pits, Rothes and Seafield, to open up Fife's deep untapped reserves. New shafts were also sunk at existing pits and optimism was high, but before these developments were ready to produce coal, the market began to shrink. Oil, nuclear power and natural gas grew in popularity and at the same time Rothes hit serious geological problems. But there was a silver lining to the gathering clouds. Two new power stations, at Kincardine and Longannet, created an assured market and to supply it a series of unspectacular-looking mines were developed.

Fife's – and Scotland's – big developments came into production in the 1960s at the same time as the market was shrinking. Old pits were closed until, by the mid-1960s, there were no deep mines left in central Fife. The closures continued through the 1970s, but despite the pain, Fife had more working pits than any other Scottish area at the time of the last great strike in 1984. Within a few years all but the Longannet complex had closed. Although its remaining production unit is just across the Clackmannanshire border, its coal all comes to Fife and the Kingdom can still claim to have a coal industry, albeit a shadow of the great undertaking that once fuelled the world.

Guthrie Hutton, 1999.

Bowhill baths were opened in July 1938 by C. Augustus Carlow, Managing Director of the Fife Coal Company, along with 82 year old Alexander McLean, a pit worker for 62 years.

Opposite: Michael Colliery, East Wemyss.

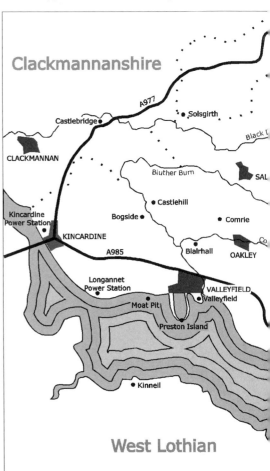

Map by Lewis Hutton.

Mary Colliery, Lochore.

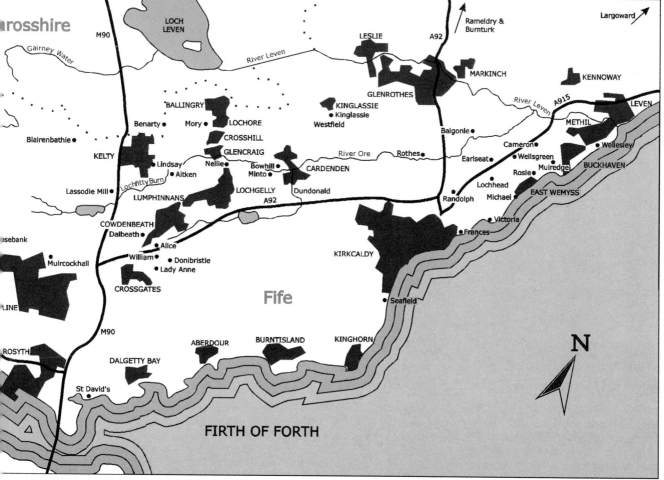

Coal was once a common sight, stacked at railway yards or on the back of a coalman's lorry, but now, although it is less familiar, we still use it. It is burned in large quantities by electricity generating stations and comes to us at the flick of a switch. Fife is Scotland's power house. The Kincardine generating station was set up in the 1950s. To the coal industry's surprise and delight, it could burn inferior coal and there was a huge, thick adjacent seam that had previously been discounted because of its poor quality. It was known as the Upper Hirst. When the Queen opened the station in October 1960 it was supplied by four main collieries, only one of which, Bogside (right), was in Fife.

Bogside mine was opened in 1959 and was operating at a profit by 1962. An output of around 1,000 tons a day had been predicted when the mine was planned but it regularly exceeded 2,000 tons and these men exceeded 3,000. In 1965 they and others, working a four shift system, produced a British record output of 3,324 tons in 24 hours, from a face 200 yards long and 4 foot 6 inches high. They also beat the mine's previous best for a week's output by 1,000 tons. It was portent of things to come from the Upper Hirst seam.

Only two years after the opening of Kincardine, the South of Scotland Electricity Board started planning another power station nearby, at Longannet. With the Grangemouth refinery just across the Forth, oil was the favoured fuel, but the National Coal Board devised an imaginative scheme which persuaded the SSEB to use coal. The idea was to open a series of drift mines into the Upper Hirst seam and deliver the coal direct to the power station by an underground conveyor – no spectacular collieries, no winding towers, no trains, just a constant stream of coal at an economic price. Work on the scheme began in 1964. This mine at Longannet was developed to bring the conveyor to the surface.

While Longannet's surface installations were unimpressive, the engineering underground was extraordinary. Working towards each other from a number of points along the line, the tunnellers had to negotiate several curved changes of gradient and still make both ends of every drivage meet precisely. Compared to the Channel Tunnel, which only worked from two ends, it was an outstanding achievement. When the complex opened, the five and a half mile conveyor belt was the longest in the world. It was 3 feet wide and could run at speeds of between 450 and 700 feet per minute, and deliver over 700 tons of coal to the surface in an hour.

The Longannet project was based on working an area of the Upper Hirst seam estimated to contain about 50 million tons. The seam was like a huge trough. It outcropped in the west near Stirling and in Fife on a line north of Culross. Its northern end was cut by a fault at the base of the Ochil Hills and it thinned out south of the Forth. In the area to be worked for Longannet the seam was broken by faults into three blocks. A mine was planned for each block. One was at Bogside where a third drift mine was opened to give access to the conveyor and open up more coal. The other mines were at Castlehill about two miles north of Bogside and at Solsgirth, a further two miles north of Castlehill. These men are driving part of the ten miles of mines and tunnel needed to develop the complex.

The two drift mines at Castlehill were driven at a dipping gradient of 1 in 4 and were completed by 1969. Coal production started in 1970 and to ensure it continued without hold-ups, roadways were driven through the coal in advance of the production faces to discover if any geological problems were likely to impede progress. The roadways were 600 feet apart and the faces highly mechanised. Conveyors delivered the coal from the faces to underground bunkers which fed the main conveyor. The total capacity of the three mines was planned at 10,000 tons a day.

Solsgirth was just across the Clackmannanshire border. It was a 'star' and regularly flew the 'league' flag as the top producer. In 1975, double-ended shearers were kept going continuously and turned out 25,260 tons from a single face in five days – a European record. There were plans to extend the conveyor from Solsgirth to Dollar, but the two mines were separated by a large fault which also limited Dollar's prospects, so the extension was never made.

The three mines worked the eastern edge of the Upper Hirst seam and in 1978 plans were approved to extend the workings to the west. The new development was just over the county border in Clackmannanshire, three miles west of Castlehill. It was called Castlebridge – 'Castle' from Castlehill and 'Bridge' from Kincardine Bridge – after a competition amongst local primary schools to find a name. The coal was at a greater depth so a pit, rather than a dipping mine, was planned to gain access to it. The shaft was designed for men and materials only because the coal would still go to Longannet by underground conveyor. It was the first pit to be sunk in Scotland for twenty years and the last NCB pit in Scotland to remain operational. It is now worked by Scottish Coal.

The Longannet complex was not the first to deliver Upper Hirst coal direct to the customer. Just along the coast, at Culross, one shaft of a remarkable late sixteenth century colliery emerged on an artificial island where ships could come alongside to load coal. Known as the Moat pit, it was developed by Sir George Bruce of Carnock in 1590. The water which inevitably got into the sub-sea pit was drained by a chain of buckets worked by a horse gin, a mechanism where horses, yoked to a central shaft, provide rotational power. The pit was abandoned in 1625 after being swamped in a storm. This 1950s drawing, with the Cleish Hills looking like the Grampians, gives some idea of what the pit might have looked like.

Blair Castle is a Georgian Mansion above Culross. The estate was bought by the Fife Coal Company during the First World War to acquire the mineral rights, and in 1927 they gave the house and 28 acres of ground to the Fife, Kinross and Clackmannan miners' welfare committee for use as a convalescent home. It was named the Charles Carlow Miners' Convalescent Home after the former Managing Director of the company. Initially the home took forty men, but was extended in the 1950s to take seventy. As the industry shrank, other homes were closed and the Carlow Home became available to men and women from all over Scotland. The attractions include dances, bus trips, snooker, bingo and, as here, bowls. The comfortable bedrooms, extensive grounds and magnificent views across the Forth make it an ideal location for rest and recuperation.

Preston Island is about three-quarters of a mile south of Valleyfield in the Firth of Forth. About 1800 Sir Robert Preston of Valleyfield House set up a complex of salt pans on the island. It was ideal: as well as being surrounded by salt water, the island had outcrops of coal. The George, Lady Anne and Eye pits produced large lumps of coal for domestic sales and a mixture of small lumps and dross, known as 'panwood', for firing the salt pans. In 1811 an explosion in the George pit caused fatalities, flooded the shaft and resulted in a reduction of salt making on the island. It was reduced further in 1823 when duties, which protected sea salt, were lifted. Unable to compete against cheaper, purer salt from Cheshire and abroad the Scottish industry declined rapidly, and by 1850 Preston Island's pans had ceased to operate. Ash deposits from Longannet power station now link the island to the shore.

The Fife Coal Company began sinking their new colliery at Low Valleyfield in 1906 and by September 1910 the two oval brick-lined shafts were completed to the Five Feet seam which, although accurately named elsewhere in Fife, was found to be seven feet thick at Valleyfield. It produced a coal that was ideal for Royal Navy ships based at nearby Rosyth. The company expected that the shafts would reach the valuable Dunfermline Splint seam – an excellent household coal – in record time, but the rock below the Five Feet seam proved to be thicker than expected.

Water, which often hampered shaft sinking, presented few problems at Valleyfield, but at 200 fathoms (a fathom is six feet and a standard unit of measure in Scottish pits) the sinkers encountered high levels of methane gas. They had to work with safety lamps for the next seventeen fathoms to get down to the Dunfermline Splint. The pit was ready to win coal by February 1911 but a month later a pocket of gas exploded, killing three men.

Men who worked in Valleyfield described it as a 'gas tank' – there was so much methane it was piped into the public gas supply. Methane is known in mining as 'firedamp'. It can explode if mixed with a certain quantity of air and ignited by a spark or flame. As well as firedamp, three other pit gases cause problems: blackdamp, or carbon dioxide, a colourless, odourless gas that can suffocate people; carbon monoxide, or whitedamp, a highly poisonous gas found in the mixture of gases present after an explosion or fire; and sulphuretted hydrogen, known as stinkdamp because it smells like rotten eggs. It is dangerous because it dulls the senses and can therefore be breathed in fatal quantities.

Valleyfield was the scene of the worst pit disaster in Fife when thirty-five men were killed by an explosion on 28th September 1939. One of the rescuers who went down had "... never seen anything like it – steel girders twisted into strange shapes; great falls of rock and debris, and men burnt beyond recognition." At the subsequent enquiry, the cause was identified as an ignition of firedamp during shot firing, but an accumulation of coal dust in some roads and insufficient stone dusting contributed to the severity of the disaster. Limestone dust had been scattered in Scottish pits following an enquiry into a disaster at Udston Colliery at Hamilton in 1887 (see front cover). The stone dust helped to damp down the coal dust and stop it from becoming airborne in an explosion, and itself exploding. Stone dust was also piled on boards suspended from the roofs of roadways. These 'barriers' were introduced in the late 1940s and were designed to drop a curtain of dust to baffle an explosion when disturbed by a blast. Stories abound of them being accidentally tipped up, covering people in white dust.

Valleyfield was reconstructed on a number of occasions. In the early 1930s output was raised to 1,200 tons a day by opening up new areas and improving the washing and screening plant. In another scheme, planned by the Fife Coal Company and implemented by the NCB, mine cars of 2 ton capacity were introduced and No. 1 headgear was adapted to raise them. As this scheme was nearing completion the NCB began work on another, more ambitious, redevelopment.

The NCB planned to raise output at Valleyfield to 3,600 tons a day by sinking a new shaft to 375 fathoms and deepening No. 2 shaft to match. The first sod of No. 3 shaft was cut on reclaimed ground to the south of the existing shafts in August 1954. The winding tower, seen here under construction, was built of pre-stressed concrete to resist corrosion from sea air. There was great concern that the development might cause subsidence in Culross, and the National Trust for Scotland sought assurances from the NCB that the historic village would be safe. They need not have worried – the shaft was never used.

Before the scheme was complete, the NCB started work on a new idea: a 3.5 mile long tunnel under the Forth to link the pit with Kinneil Colliery at Bo'ness. The tunnellers met in the middle on 30th April 1964, some months before the much trumpeted Forth Road Bridge was completed and the mining community took some pride in beating the bridge builders across the Forth. The output of the two collieries was concentrated on the preparation plant at Kinneil, although some of Valleyfield's coal still came up in Fife. The link gave the two pits a new lease of life and Valleyfield stayed in production until closure in 1978.

The extensive pit bottom of Valleyfield No. 3.

Torry Mine, to the north of Valleyfield, was completed in the mid-1950s after four years of development. It was linked to Valleyfield by a new railway which included a half-mile long tunnel and a bridge over the Bluther Burn. It also had a short road tunnel which is seen here under construction and being crossed by an Alexander's 'Bluebird' bus. Torry was one of a number of short-term drift mines opened by the NCB. They were set up in areas of known coal reserves and normally took only about two years to develop. The Coal Board needed them to help meet the desperate post-war fuel shortage because a lot of old pits had to close before the big developments like Rothes and Seafield would be ready. The mines were also useful as a way of employing skilled men, displaced from old pits, until there were jobs for them at the new developments.

Torry was designed to produce about 400 tons of coal a day. Cars of coal or debris were drawn out of the mine by rope haulage. They were then hauled by diesel locomotives along the new railway, seen here at the Bluther Burn. The cars were tipped into one of three bunkers at Valleyfield: one took saleable coal, another was for boiler fuel and the third for waste. Pit waste at Valleyfield was tipped on the foreshore and over many years it created a peninsular that projected into Firth of Forth toward Preston Island. Torry closed in 1965.

Blairhall Colliery, to the north of Valleyfield, was developed in the 1870s by the Carron Iron Company to win blackband ironstone. There were two principal shafts, both 90 fathoms deep, and an older ironstone shaft of 80 fathoms. Carron worked the pit for about eight years before selling it to the Lochgelly Iron Company who in turn sold it to the Coltness Iron Company, one of Scotland's dominant iron and coal concerns. As well as ironstone the pit worked Parrot coal (so called because of the chattering noise it made when burning) but by the late 1890s both were nearing exhaustion. Instead of giving up on the pit, however, the Coltness Iron Company sank two new shafts to work 1,500 tons of coal a day from the Jersey, Mynheer, Glassee, Five Feet and Dunfermline Splint seams. The shafts were about 200 yards from the old ones, 61 feet apart and 340 fathoms deep. They were named 'Lord Bruce' and 'Lady Veronica' after Lord Elgin's son and daughter.

Sinking of the original shafts had been hampered by water, but the new shafts were expected to remain dry because of the draining effect the old workings would have on them. It was therefore a bit of a surprise when 200 gallons a minute started pouring in at the 24 fathom level and large pumps were needed to keep the water under control. Although it was wet and very gassy, Blairhall almost lived up to expectations. In 1906, when the new shafts were begun, the company estimated its life at about seventy years; they were nearly right as it closed in 1969.

Inset: The miners' welfare fund was set up under the Mining Industries Act of 1920. It was raised by a levy of one penny a week from miners, and a similar levy on the owners for every ton of coal produced. The money had to be spent in the areas where it was raised and local committees were set up to determine what it was spent on. The Fife, Kinross and Clackmannan committee decided to build institutes and associated facilities and Fife's first was opened at Blairhall in May 1924 by R.W. Wallace, chairman of the committee. Institutes like this became a focal point for mining communities as can be seen with this group at Blairhall.

Scotland's coal industry reached its peak in 1913 when over 42 million tons were mined. In the difficult years that followed many pits closed and there was little investment in the industry. The gloom was lifted on 25th July 1935 when the first sod of the Fife Coal Company's new Comrie pit was cut. It incorporated a number of European and American concepts, new to mining in Scotland, as if the industry had skipped a developmental generation and was starting afresh. Comrie was so new and different it was described by Home Secretary, Herbert Morrison MP, as the 'Cat's Pyjamas'. The fountain and pond was part of the cooling system for the man-winding shaft braking system, but almost inevitably it became a symbol of the pit's modernity. It also brought out ancient survival instincts in the local seagulls – they ate the goldfish. Managers raided their own ponds and fish tanks to replenish the stocks, but the grisly carnage went on!

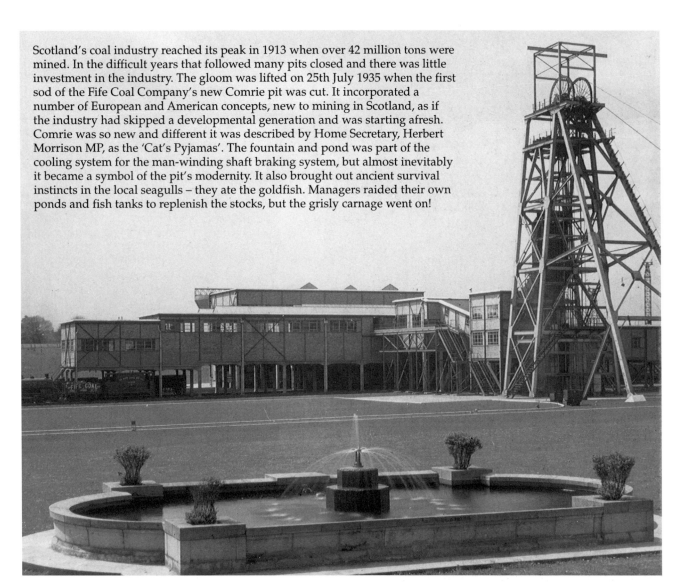

The pit was set in open country a mile from the Comrie to Saline road. No. 1 shaft was sunk to a depth of 214 fathoms and equipped for raising coal in skips. No. 2 shaft was 208 fathoms and intended for men and materials. It was also used as the ventilation downcast shaft. Unusually, the pit had a forcing fan to push air into the pit rather than the more usual practice of drawing it through with an extractor fan. Comrie was expected to employ 400 men within five years of its opening and 1,000 in ten years. But before it went into full production, the country was at war again and the company was never able to bask in the full glory of their achievement.

Left: The flat-roofed, brick, pithead buildings at Comrie were fine examples of 1930s industrial architecture. The last to be completed were the baths which were opened in June 1942 by former miner Tom Smith MP, Parliamentary Secretary to the new Ministry of Fuel, Light and Power. The joke in the Comrie baths was that you could tell the area a man worked in because Bankhead men had webbed feet! The Bankhead area was wet whereas Langfaulds was hot and stoorie.

As well as washing the men, collieries had facilities to wash and sort the coal before it was sent to customers. Construction men are seen here working inside the washery cone which was used to separate slurry from the water. The preparation and washing plant was capable of cleaning all of the pit's daily output, initially estimated at 4,000 tons although the best the pit achieved was 3,260 tons in August 1969.

Below, left: An aerial ropeway, seen here looking out across the washery cone, removed debris from the pit and preparation plant. It could deposit up to 180 tons an hour on the bing.

When clean air policies were adopted in the 1960s, coal faced a problem because natural smokeless fuels, like anthracite was unsuitable for domestic grates. An alternative was needed and the Scottish Rexco Company built a plant alongside Comrie designed to convert 100,000 tons of coal a year into domestic smokeless fuel. It was opened in January 1964 by long-serving Comrie miner, Thomas Sutherland.

Below: The coal was worked by a method known as longwall retreating, in which roads are driven to the boundary of the area to be worked and the coal extracted as the miners work back toward the shaft. Diesel locomotives operating on level roads hauled trains of mine cars of 3.5 tons capacity. It took the contents of three cars to fill a skip, which was then raised to the surface. In 1980 Comrie held an open day to celebrate the fortieth anniversary of the start of coal production. Six years later, the pit was closed.

An old mineral railway, which connected the defunct Oakley Collieries' Kinneddar pit to the main line, was used to develop Comrie pit and new sidings were laid out at Oakley. It had been hoped to build a bridge over the A907 Alloa to Dunfermline road, but it was never done and this level crossing at Comrie village caused traffic hold-ups throughout the pit's life. On at least one occasion the hold-up lasted for over half an hour when the shunter forgot to re-open the gates. The NCB 'pug' No. 7 (small colliery locomotives were known as pugs) taking trucks to the Oakley sidings here, was built in Staffordshire for the War Department in 1945. She was taken over by the NCB in 1963 and spent most of her Coal Board life at Comrie.

Accommodation at Oakley was needed for miners and their families, but war interrupted house building. A materials and labour shortage after the war meant that a number of 'prefabs' (prefabricated houses) like these in Wardlaw Way were erected. Nearly 150,000 were built throughout Britain. They were intended as a short term solution to the desperate housing shortage, but some lasted for a long time. A number of types were developed; these houses were of aluminium, coated with bitumen and cement, and were made at aircraft factories struggling to find a post-war role – many were built at the Blackburn factory in Dumbarton. They had a mass-produced service core with a kitchen and bathroom which was a great improvement on the old miners' rows. Although they were small and had condensation problems, many people were sorry to leave the prefabs when permanent homes became available.

Rosebank Colliery at Parkneuk, to the north west of Dunfermline, was operated by John Nimmo & Sons of Glasgow. It was a large concern employing, in 1914, over 300 men underground and 50 on the surface. At that time it was worked by four shafts: Nos. 2 and 3 were operated together while No. 1 was worked separately, as was this more isolated No. 6 or 'Wallsend' shaft. Wallsend was an old name for the Dunfermline Splint seam. Another of the Rosebank pits, the 'Dixie', had its engine house and other pithead buildings destroyed by fire in 1900.

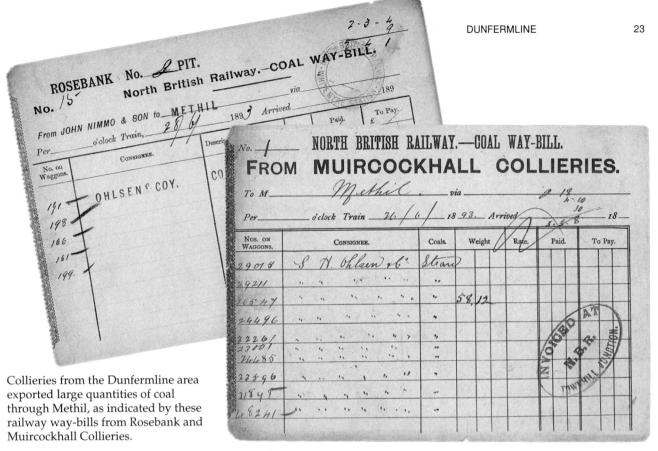

Collieries from the Dunfermline area exported large quantities of coal through Methil, as indicated by these railway way-bills from Rosebank and Muircockhall Collieries.

Muircockhall pit, in the Townhill area of Dunfermline, was operated by Henry Ness & Company. Mining ceased in July 1943 as part of a scheme to concentrate wartime output on the most productive pits, but while wartime circumstances closed it, they also kept it going – as a training pit. In 1943, the Minister of Labour, Ernest Bevin, sought to solve the serious manpower shortage in the coal industry by introducing a scheme whereby every tenth conscript was sent to work in the pits – even though some of them had trained in cadet forces and were willing to fight. They were called Bevin Boys and many were trained at Muircockhall. After the war it remained as a training pit – this group of recruits, some in army battle dress, was photographed in 1946.

Outcrops were first worked on Fordell Estate in the sixteenth century and coal was carried in horse-borne panniers to Inverkeithing for shipping. These transport arrangements restricted mining development until the 1750s when Sir Robert Henderson constructed St David's harbour and laid a wooden waggonway to it. It was one of the earliest railways in Scotland. In 1781, Sir Robert was succeeded by his son, Sir John. At that time water was threatening to halt production at the mines and so he had a tunnel cut, 20 fathoms below the surface, to carry water from them to the Fordell Burn. It was known as the Fordell Day Level and was a remarkable piece of mining engineering.

Fordell pits had distinctive names like Humbug, Bulwark, Vengeance, Vulnerable, Lady Anne and George. The William pit, originally known as the Wellington, was sunk in 1843 to 75 fathoms. Its initial link with the Fordell Railway was an inclined plane worked by gravity – full waggons going down the incline pulled empty ones back up. A connection with the Fordell Railway was made in 1872. 'Old Father William' closed in 1950.

The Alice pit near Hill of Beath was sunk beside the main North British Railway in 1880, but did not go into production until 1894 when a connection was laid across Mossmorran to the Fordell Railway. It produced a high quality coal. The headgear and screening plant were reconstructed by the Blantyre Engineering Company between June and September 1926.

The Henderson Mine was begun in 1946 and opened in 1948. It was intended as a drawing mine for the William and Alice pits. Instead of raising old hutches in the shafts, the idea was to cut the coal by machine and draw it to the surface in large capacity mine cars.

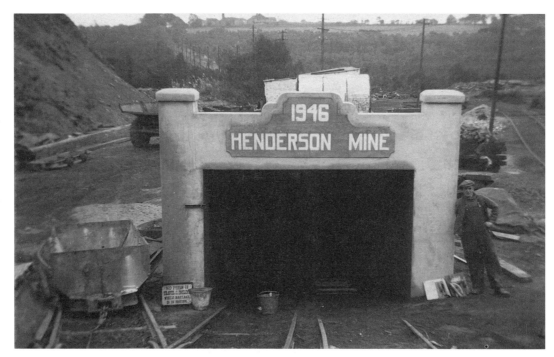

The Fordell Railway was 4.5 inches narrower than standard gauge railways so the Alice pit sidings had to be laid with three rails to accommodate both main line and Fordell locomotives and rolling stock. This meant that the output of the Alice and neighbouring George pits could be transported by either railway. By the end of the Second World War less than 10% of Fordell coal was being sent to St David's harbour, so it was closed, along with much of the railway, in August 1946. Coal from the Lady Anne and William pits was sent up the line in Fordell waggons to the Alice pit where it was transferred into standard gauge railway trucks for onward transit. Operations at Fordell ceased in 1966.

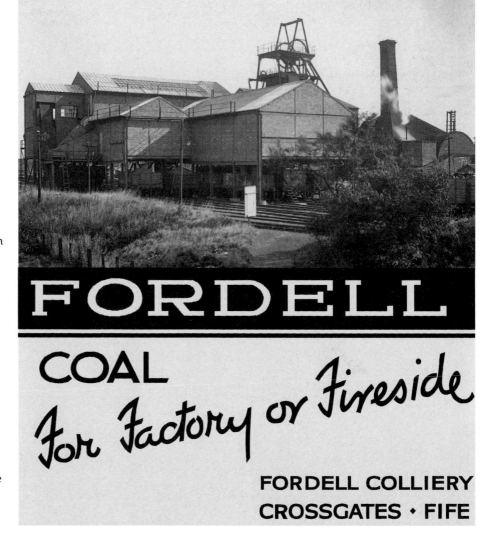

The coal industry returned to St David's harbour in 1955 when this drilling rig was assembled there. It was needed to provide information about the undersea reserves of the new Seafield Colliery at Kirkcaldy. Engineers, who had made sea forts during the Second World War, designed it to drill to 2,000 feet below the sea bed. The 185 foot high rig was able to withstand winds of up to 80 m.p.h. and stand firm in 30 foot waves. It had living accommodation for twenty-five men. It was floated out of the shallow harbour mouth on a high spring tide and three tugs towed it to Kirkcaldy. A burned-out generator coil delayed the setting up and it was late at night before it finally settled on the sea bed.

The building of St David's harbour was a precursor of later, much bigger, dock developments for shipping Fife coal to other parts of the world. One of these developments was at Burntisland where two docks, with a combined deep water area of 17 acres, were built. Each dock had six coal hoists with loading capacities of 200 tons – two of them can be seen in this view of the busy East Dock. It could take ships with a beam of 60 feet and a draught of over 28 feet.

Much of the coal from west and central Fife pits was shipped at Burntisland. Here steam coal from Cowdenbeath has been loaded into the hold of the 2,472 ton *Terneuzen*, a collier from London. The Greenock-built ship had a 44 foot beam and would therefore have loaded her cargo in the East Dock.

Although Burntisland did not have a coal industry of its own, it was where Fife's largest shale oil industry was sited. The mines and oilworks were just inland from the town at Binnend and operated between 1878 and 1901.

"Pit life would be agreeable enough if all the miners' dwellings were as picturesque as those of Donibristle and Fordell," wrote a *Glasgow Herald* reporter in 1907. In comparing mining communities in Fife with those of his native Lanarkshire he found depressing similarities in Lochgelly and Cowdenbeath, but was clearly charmed by the two little villages. He wrote of " . . . daintily curtained windows . . . " and " . . . trim rows, gay with flowers as though they were the abode of gardeners, rather than colliers". This view of Donibristle (top) certainly looks different from the miners' rows of the west.

Above: Hill of Beath Estate, with its colliery and fireclay works, was bought by the Fife Coal Company in 1887. The small collection of houses quickly expanded into a company village of over 200 houses and a population of nearly 1,200 people. The company also built a hall and reading room and, in 1896, the first Gothenburg-style pub in Scotland (see page 44).

Dalbeath was the main coal-winning unit for Hill of Beath Colliery. The large rectangular shaft was divided into three sections: one for pumping and two for winding. The winding engines and headgear were mounted alongside each other.

HILL OF BEATH DISASTER

1901 was a bad year for accidents. In February seven men were overcome by carbon monoxide poisoning from a fire at the Hill of Beath Colliery's Engine Pit. The fire, in the Lochgelly Splint and Parrot Coal seam, had first broken out in July 1900. It had been sealed to stop air reaching it, but had continued to burn and was sealed again in December. Two months later two men went to inspect it but when they failed to return, the manager and five men went to find them. Realising they were in danger they turned back, but were overcome by gas. Four died. More search parties went down and another man was lost before company officials arrived to take charge of the situation.

DONIBRISTLE DISASTER

Donibristle was one of the oldest and best appointed collieries in Fife. It was operated by the Donibristle Colliery Company and worked coal under Mossmorran moorland. At about one o'clock on the afternoon of 26th August 1901, two men drove up through the rock roof and a liquid mass of peat and water poured into the pit. Eleven men were trapped. Two rescue parties were formed and one man was saved, but four rescuers failed to return – fourteen men were now trapped. On the surface a huge crater had formed. Peat was still running into the pit so men started to dig rescue shafts. They worked all night, but the soft ground and water forced them to give up. The only way to reach the trapped men was through the opening in the crater. Working under the direction of the manager of Bowhill Colliery, men erected boards round the opening and improvised a cage. It was lowered into the pit and six men were found. Five were brought out before the boarding broke under the weight of water and peat. The sixth man and two of his rescuers were now trapped but the following morning, Robert Law, a miner from Cowdenbeath, went down alone and brought them out. Attempts to rescue the other eight men had to be abandoned; their bodies were recovered later.

The Hill of Beath and Donibristle disasters happened before an organised rescue service had been established and those who had risked their lives to save others had done so as untrained volunteers. There was never any shortage of men willing to put their lives on the line when others were in peril – that was the way it was in mining communities.

The Coal Mines Act of 1911 made it compulsory for coal owners' associations to set up rescue stations to train men in rescue techniques, but the Fife and Clackmannan Coalowners' Association beat the legislators. They established Scotland's first rescue station at Stenhouse Street, Cowdenbeath, in 1910. The first superintendent was David Stevenson, a first-aider from Bowhill Colliery. He is on the left, resplendent in moustache and cap, with this unidentified team. The men are wearing W.E.G. breathing apparatus (named after its inventor, William E. Garforth) which mixed oxygen with purified exhaled air.

The Fife owners' early lead was not followed by others who delayed setting up a rescue service until a universally accepted breathing system was adopted. It was a delay that could have cost lives. In 1913 this rescue team from Bowhill Colliery were called to a fire at Cadder pit near Glasgow. They were so far out of their territory that they had to ask a policeman in Kirkintilloch for directions. Despite taking a long time to get there, they managed to bring one man out who would almost certainly have died if trained men had not given assistance.

Cowdenbeath was a 'B scheme' station – one that trained teams of part-time brigadesmen from individual collieries and co-ordinated rescue operations. Teams consisted of five to eight men and every colliery, or group of collieries, employing up to 500 men had to have a team while the larger collieries had more than one.

The Cowdenbeath Coal Company operated a number of shafts over a large area. In the early 1890s Cowdenbeath No. 7 was the ventilation downcast and pumping shaft for the whole colliery, with No. 3 as the upcast and No. 8 as a pumping and downcast shaft. No. 9 shaft had been sunk by 1896 when the company was taken over by the Fife Coal Company who then sank No. 10 shaft. Fifty years later, at the time of nationalisation, No. 7 was the only coal-producing shaft, with No. 10 being used for pumping and ventilation. The colliery closed in January 1960.

Mossbeath pit was sunk by the Cowdenbeath Coal Company in the 1890s, before being taken over by the Fife Coal Company. It had two shafts, 45 feet apart. No. 1 was rectangular and equipped with pumps and a double-decked cage while No. 2 was 10 feet square and used with a single decked cage. The pumps were able to clear 312 gallons of water a minute from a depth of nearly 67 fathoms. In the 1930s the pit was reorganised, as seen here, with a single working shaft and linked to Cowdenbeath No. 10. The ventilation system was also reorganised at the same time. A fire closed the colliery in 1945, although one shaft was maintained for training purposes.

Opposite: Over time, equipment became more sophisticated but canaries remained part of the rescue man's armoury. The little birds were quickly affected by gas, giving early warning of its presence (although they too had their own breathing apparatus known as the Haldane Cage). Rescue training was rigorous and only the fittest men were accepted. Following the explosion at the Lindsay Colliery in 1957, Cowdenbeath became the first station in Britain to have alarm bells fitted in brigadesmen's houses so that they could be called out quickly in an emergency. Rescuers also attended incidents outside mines, such as the collapse of the Masterton flyover at Inverkeithing in 1962. With the rapid contraction of the industry in the 1980s, Fife's rescue station became the last in Scotland. It was privatised and moved to Crossgates where it operates as a training agency, specialising in safety and rescue in confined spaces. The men also have to respond, within an hour, to emergencies at Castlebridge pit.

Kirkford Pit. Cowdenbeath.

Cowdenbeath No. 10 was also known as Kirkford pit. In July 1907 three men, including eighteen year old William Ostler, were preparing for the restart after the holidays. They were 'redding' (clearing) a roof fall when another fall buried them. Helped by the struggles of one his colleagues, Ostler broke free. The fall had also extinguished the lights so, in total blackness, he found their pony and set out to get help. The pony led him to the stables, but went into its stall and stayed there. The young man then followed a hutch rail to the shaft bottom. The pit-bottomer was working on the surface when he heard repeated signalling and descended to find Ostler lying next to the 400 foot deep shaft, his face covered in blood from bad head injuries. He was taken to the surface and a rescue party went to help his companions, one of whom died soon after being found. There was admiration for Ostler's heroism and astonishment that such a badly injured man could have travelled so far in the dark, negotiating numerous ventilation trap-doors along the way. But his effort had taken its toll. He collapsed into semi-consciousness the following day and died five days later.

Foulford No. 1 was another Cowdenbeath Coal Company pit taken over by the Fife Coal Company. The main shaft was about a mile to the east of Cowdenbeath Station and was used for winding, pumping and ventilation downcast. The ventilation upcast No. 2 shaft was about 200 yards away. There was a large brickworks alongside which produced about 20,000 pressed bricks a day in the 1890s. Foulford was shut down temporarily in the 1920s and finally closed in 1931.

Gordon pit, to the south of Foulford, was worked between 1893 and 1939. Along with the Dora and Lochhead pits and Lochhead mine, it formed the Little Raith Collieries. Dora was the last working pit of the group when it ceased production at the end of February 1959. When it closed it had an annual output of 66,000 tons and had been producing coal for over 100 years. On the last coal-producing shift a heavy roof-fall in the Fourteen Feet section trapped a 65 year old miner, but he was released by a workmate. Like many pits in the area the Gordon seams outcropped. Miners were able to make holes to the surface and come up for a smoke, and something to eat, before returning to their subterranean toil.

Cowdenbeath Central Works and Offices were set up by the Fife Coal Company in 1924. At the time a central workshops for such a large group of pits was unusual. They contained offices, a laboratory, engineering works and stores and when the NCB took them over, they employed 750 people. In the early days the workshops concentrated on repairs and maintenance of anything from coal cutter picks to steam locomotives. In time, however, they made a wide variety of equipment including mine cars, waggon springs and elevator buckets. The NCB used the Cowdenbeath operation as the Area Offices and Central Works for their Fife and Clackmannan Area. The works were visited by King George VI and Queen Elizabeth, the Queen Mother, in June 1948 and they became the only workshops for Fife when the Dysart and Alloa workshops closed in 1967. They remained as the last working remnant of Cowdenbeath's great coal industry until closure in 1988.

Strikes, or lock-outs, in the mining industry were often bitter, protracted affairs. Communities faced long periods of hardship, but they faced them together. They set up soup kitchens, like this at Broad Street School in 1921, to provide food for hungry people. Manning it from left to right are: George Pritchard, Miss Boyd, John Renton, Nettie Hately, unknown, Mrs Boyd, Robert Murdoch, unknown, James Laing, Provost Russell, John McFarlane, Mrs Russell, David Guthrie, unknown, Mrs Cunningham, Andrew Cunningham, Miss Russell and John Shedden.

The 1921 strike brought trouble and troops to Cowdenbeath. Miners marched to pits to stop managers from firing the boilers. At Dalbeath they abducted a Fife Coal Company general manager, William Spalding, and marched him through the town before he was rescued by police. One man was arrested. He was imprisoned two days later and his supporters broke windows and street lamps in protest, an action condemned by the Union. For a week Cowdenbeath was peaceful, but then soldiers and marines moved in, and the police made more arrests. Troops guarded the pits while company officials kept the boilers fired and the pumps working. The strike ended in defeat for the miners four months later.

The imposing Miners' Welfare Institute in Broad Street was opened in 1928. It became the focus for the mining community in times of trouble, but the intensity of the disputes of 1921 and 1926 was not repeated until the last great national strike in 1984.

A Row of Colliers' Houses, Cowdenbeath.

The community spirit that set up the soup kitchens had its roots in the rows of houses that typified mining communities. In small villages and larger towns like Cowdenbeath, the rows, like this one in Broad Street, were the same: one or two storey buildings of no architectural merit, usually made of cheap brick and built together to save money on gable walls. The houses were tiny, with one or two rooms and no proper sanitation. The occupants of up to four houses had to share outside toilets and wash houses, and each housewife had an allocated day to do the family wash. By present standards the rows were cramped, damp little hovels, but the shared experience of privation and poverty engendered a neighbourliness that would be almost impossible to recreate today. The loss of that spirit, if not the buildings, is sad.

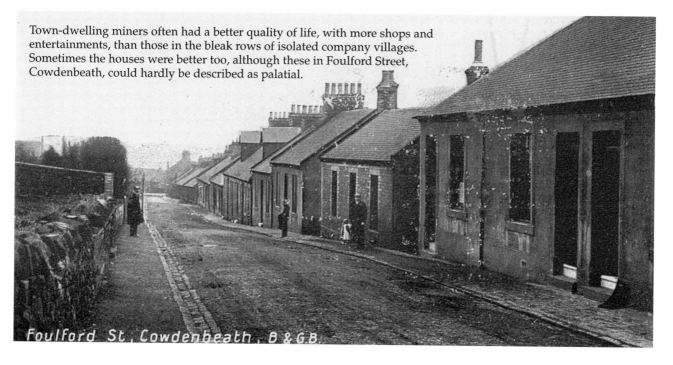

Town-dwelling miners often had a better quality of life, with more shops and entertainments, than those in the bleak rows of isolated company villages. Sometimes the houses were better too, although these in Foulford Street, Cowdenbeath, could hardly be described as palatial.

Foulford St, Cowdenbeath. B & G.B.

Scottish mining men learned their skills at educational establishments like the Heriot Watt School of Mining in Edinburgh, the Royal Technical College in Glasgow and the Fife Mining School in Cowdenbeath. Fife's school was originally set up in two rooms of the Broad Street School in 1895, moving from there in 1910 to the basement of the new Beath High School. The picture shows the school's electrical laboratory in 1915. Embarrassingly for a mining school, Beath High School began to sink, despite having been built on what was thought to be a safe site. It was examined by a Royal Commission on mining subsidence in 1925 who regarded it as one of the worst examples in Fife.

FIFE MINING SCHOOL, BROAD STREET, COWDENBEATH

Although Beath High School remained in use, shored up and held together with tie bars, a new mining school was built in Broad Street. The Miners' Welfare Commission donated £16,000 for its construction and it was opened in March 1935 by the Minister for Mines, Ernest Brown MP. It had spacious accommodation including mechanical and electrical workshops and rooms for planning and drawing. The school closed in 1976.

COWDENBEATH FOOTBALL CLUB

Mining men enjoyed football and their teams competed at all levels which, for Cowdenbeath FC, meant some time at the top. The 'Miners', as they were known, won promotion to the First Division in 1924 and stayed there for ten years. Their home ground, Central Park, was an impressive amphitheatre with a good view (!) of No. 7 pit. The stand could hold 3,500 spectators and the terraces, built up with colliery waste, could hold many more. Relegation in 1934 ended Cowdenbeath's time at the top although they won the Second Division Championship in 1939 and who knows what might have happened if the war had not prevented promotion! This team from the second half of the 1930s is: *back row* – Clark (Capt.) Rougvie, Scott, Wilkie, Deans and Gorrie; *front row* – Eadie, Guthrie, Graham, McCurley and Boag. In more recent years Cowdenbeath has become better known as the 'Blue Brazil' although being 'Miners' was easier to understand!

Football offered young men the chance to escape from pit life and perhaps these lads were dreaming of fame when they posed in front of a spoil heap in the Cowdenbeath/Kelty area. Fifers who 'escaped' include John Thomson, the Celtic goalkeeper who was tragically killed in a game against Rangers in 1931. Before joining the Glasgow club he played with Bowhill Rovers and Wellesley Juniors. The Rangers and Scotland hero, 'Slim' Jim Baxter, worked at Fordell Colliery before he turned professional. He started playing with Crossgates Primrose, one of many clubs from mining areas with names like Heatherbell, Rose and Violet – delicate blooms that hardly matched their style of play!

Dunfermline company Thomas Spowart & Co. operated the Lassodie Collieries, a nest of pits to the north of the town. It was a big operation, employing over 750 people at the start of the First World War. The Lassodie Mill Colliery, near Kelty, was a separate operation belonging to the Rosewell Gas Coal Company. It was taken over by the Fife Coal Company in 1905, about the time this picture was taken. The miners are all wearing tallow or 'tally' lamps in their caps. Tally lamps had a reservoir which the men filled with seal oil or stuffed with wax. A wick from the reservoir was led through a spout and it burned with a yellow, smoky flame.

Work began on developing Blairenbathie Colliery, to the west of Kelty, in 1895. The two shafts were sunk to 112 fathoms. The pit was taken over by the newly formed Fife and Kinross Coal Company in 1897 which in turn was taken over by the Fife Coal Company in 1901. The workings were badly affected by faults and intrusions and the colliery was shut down during a slump in trade in 1925. It closed the following year during the miners' strike.

Blairenbathie Mine was developed by
the Fife Coal Company in 1945/46
close to the site of the old pit. Serious
problems were encountered with
water during development and the old
pit's geological troubles dogged the
new mine too. It closed in 1962.

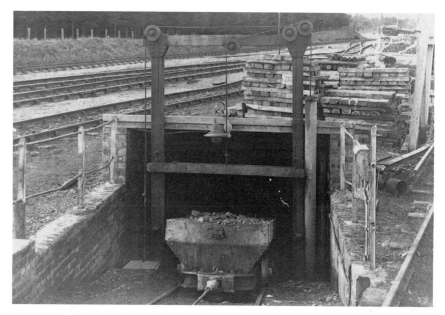

The NCB's policy of opening drift
mines in the late 1940s and early 50s to
fill the production gap was based on
the Fife Coal Company's Benarty Mine
near Kelty. Before the Second World
War, company officials had visited
America and seen shallow mines
which "took the railway down the
pit". When wartime Britain needed
coal in a hurry the company was able
to put a scheme, based on this idea,
into practice by enlarging and
redeveloping an existing pair of
ventilation mines at Benarty. The mine
was not intended to have a long life,
but was expected to go into
production quickly and be a high
producer. Work began in September
1944 and the first coal was drawn the
following March. Within a year, 350
tons a week was being produced at a
rate, per man-shift, three times the
Scottish average.

The railway, as such, was not taken
down Benarty mine, but narrow-gauge
rails were laid into it for the operation
of drop-bottom mine cars. These were
hauled up on to a gantry and
unloaded into two 15 ton hoppers. The
coal was then taken by lorry to the
washer at Aitken Colliery. Benarty
Mine closed in 1959.

Lindsay Pit, Kelty

Sinking of Kelty Nos. 4 and 5 began in 1874. They were the first shafts sunk by the Fife Coal Company and were later named Lindsay Colliery after the company's first chairman, William Lindsay. The two shafts were 15 feet apart and went down to the Lochgelly Splint seam at 71 fathoms. The 'wee pit', as No. 5 was known, stayed at that depth but No. 4 shaft was enlarged in 1886 and deepened to the Dunfermline Splint seam at 130 fathoms. The pithead, seen here about 1913, was reconstructed after a fire in 1919. Two surface mines were also opened in association with the main colliery in 1924 and 1939.

On 14th December 1957 nine men were killed and eleven injured by an explosion in the Glassee No. 3 section; one of the men was overcome by gas trying to rescue others. The enquiry concluded that a match, struck to light a cigarette, was the cause. At the time not all pits were regarded as dangerous and some were still being worked by miners using naked flame lamps, but Lindsay was not one of them. Two previous explosions at the pit, in 1929 and 1955, had resulted in one fatality and so Lindsay was designated as a 'safety lamp pit' where cigarettes and matches were known as 'contraband' and banned.

This picture of the reconstructed Lindsay is in marked contrast to the earlier view. A more modern looking Kelty has also replaced the old miners' rows on the left – only Benarty Hill seems unchanged! The 'Grand Old Lady' closed in January 1965.

The shed-like building on the left of the picture on the opposite page housed the picking tables. This picture on the right shows what it was like inside sometime in the 1890s. When coal came up from below it had to be graded, picked clean of any stones and washed before it could be sent to customers. Picking was often done by 'pit-head lassies'. After women were banned from undergound work in 1842, many continued to be employed on the surface as pickers.

On 24 March 1893 the first sod of the Fife Coal Company's Aitken Colliery was cut at a spot about 1,100 yards north-east of Lindsay Colliery. It was named after the company chairman, Thomas Aitken of Nivingston. There was much celebrating and drinking of toasts, which apparently left some of the guests struggling to keep their feet (and perhaps their dignity) on the line of planks from the marquee to the station! Sinking proper began in July and a single, rectangular, timber-lined shaft, topped with brick, was sunk to the Dunfermline Splint seam at 207 fathoms. A level mine, driven from the Lindsay, linked the two pits together and satisfied the legal requirement for all pits to have two means of escape.

The Fife Coal Company, Ltd.
Aitken Pit and Power Station.

Safety Slogan No. 3

Share your safety experience
with your neighbour—don't let
him suffer through inexperience.

No. 611

The cages were running to the Lochgelly Splint early in 1896 and by 1897 the pit was producing 1,000 tons a day. Two years later a fire broke out in the engine house and spread to the haulage and screening houses. Prompt action stopped the cage from falling down the shaft while the men in the pit escaped through the Lindsay. After the First World War, surface installations and the washery were reconstructed, and a new No. 2 shaft was sunk to 95 fathoms. A power station was also built which at the time was the largest colliery station in Scotland, supplying electricity to thirteen of the company's pits. It also provided ash for spreading on icy roads in winter. The wooden cooling towers on the left were replaced by concrete ones in 1948.

One of the main seams worked at the Aitken was known as the Glassee (Glass eye?), one of the most prized coals of the Fife coalfield. It was found in the Aitken No. 1 shaft at a depth of 160 fathoms, was 4.5 feet thick and dipped at an angle of about 1 in 2. The steepness of the dip is shown in this picture of the Glassee seam taken in 1929.

The Fife Coal Company, Ltd.

Aitken Pit and Power Station.

Safety Slogan No. 5

One accident may be one too many—it might be your last.

No. 591

These tubs, or hutches, at the Aitken pit bottom are chalked with messages to identify their contents. One is prominently marked 'redd', a Scots word meaning debris. The same word, as a verb, describes the act of clearing up which was done in the pits by a reddsman. On the surface, the debris was tipped on the redd bing ('bing' means heap or pile in old Scots). Many Scots words survived in common usage in the mining industry, with regional variations from Fife to Ayrshire. More than an industry was lost when mining ceased!

Aitken Colliery was brought to a standstill in 1907 by a dispute over weighing. The company had introduced a machine called 'Billy Fairplay', which allowed them to separate dross from coal and only pay miners for coal, instead of the number of hutches they had filled. After a three-week strike the company agreed to a fairer system. Aitken went on to become a model of consistency, producing just under 2,000 tons a day. It closed in 1963.

The big mining companies opposed the granting of pub licenses in their towns and villages until the Industrial and Providential Societies Act was passed in 1893. This allowed pubs to be set up as co-operative ventures with profits used to provide community improvements. Buildings were austere, interiors uninviting, credit was not allowed, and gambling and games (even dominoes) were prohibited. Management was 'disinterested' and did not promote the sale of drink; men could drink if they wanted to, but the community would benefit, not the landlord. It was a Swedish idea, so the pubs were called Gothenburgs – Goths for short. Fife embraced the idea more than any other part of Scotland and the first Goth was set up by the Fife Coal Company at Hill of Beath in 1896. Others followed – the Kelty Public House Society operated four. No. 1 Goth, seen above, was on the corner of High Street and Station Road while No. 2 Goth was on the opposite corner across the High Street.

Gothenburg Hall, Kelty.

There was a strong temperance element to the Goth idea, but it didn't really work. One pub customer, interviewed in 1907, felt proud of his achievements: he and his fellow drinkers had provided a district nurse, a hall and Saturday evening concerts. These were staged as a counter attraction to the pub, but to ensure that the concerts kept going there had to be an attraction for them to be a counter attraction to, so he kept on drinking! One of those halls was in Kelty High Street, next to No. 2 Goth beside the terminus for the Dunfermline trams. A clock tower was added in 1925. The hall showed films and provided stiff competition for the Regal cinema next door.

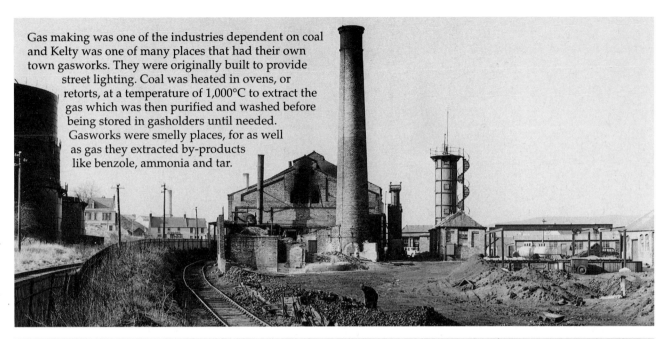

Gas making was one of the industries dependent on coal and Kelty was one of many places that had their own town gasworks. They were originally built to provide street lighting. Coal was heated in ovens, or retorts, at a temperature of 1,000°C to extract the gas which was then purified and washed before being stored in gasholders until needed. Gasworks were smelly places, for as well as gas they extracted by-products like benzole, ammonia and tar.

Lumphinnans No. 11 was south-east of Kelty. It was normally identified with Roman numerals – No. XI – and known locally as the 'peesweep' (a Scots' word for the lapwing which is often given as a name to pits or miners' rows in country areas). It was a new pit when the Fife Coal Company took it over from the Cowdenbeath Coal Company in 1896. Ten years later two men were overcome by whitedamp (carbon monoxide) after a fire in the Parrot Coal seam. This tragedy is also remembered for the actions of the company's future chairman, C. Augustus Carlow, who led the rescue party carrying a caged canary from his kitchen. When the bird showed signs of distress he ordered a retreat – such was the rudimentary nature of mines rescue before the service was set up. A new No. 12 (or No. XII) shaft was sunk in the mid-1920s and a new washery installed in 1928. Pit-head baths for 608 men were provided in 1933 and the NCB carried out further reconstruction in the 1950s. The pit closed in November 1966.

These back to back rows at Lumphinnans, with their communal washing 'green', were built on the site of an old ironworks next to a brickworks and Lumphinnans No. 1 pit. Women trying to keep washing clean next to a working pit faced an uphill struggle against grit and grime from the colliery chimney.

Lumphinnans No. 1 Colliery was sunk as an ironstone pit in 1852. It was taken over in 1883 by the Cowdenbeath Coal Company and in 1896 by the Fife Coal Company. Although the main No. 1 shaft was 180 fathoms deep, coal working was apparently concentrated on the upper levels until the 1920s when lower levels down to the Dunfermline Splint were opened out. The pit was closed in 1957.

In times of hardship, like the prolonged strikes of 1912 and the 1920s, people from mining communities scavenged for coal. They scoured pit bings for any that had been thrown away and dug to find outcrops near the surface, which appears to be what a Crossgates photographer has recorded here, although the place and date are unknown. During the 1921 strike some Lochgelly men, digging on high ground to the north of the Loch, found Lochgelly Splint coal. A trench was opened up and people came from all over the area to dig or help. The excavation was well organised. Men worked at 'the face', while others threw the coal up to the surface. There it was gathered by women, children and older men who loaded it into sacks to be taken to town by cart. There was enough coal for everyone, although for every bag a man filled for his own family's use, he had to fill one for the soup kitchen as well. Any surplus was sold for soup kitchen funds.

Lochgelly's Miners' Welfare institute was one of many in Fife that were improved and upgraded in the early 1950s. Bowling greens and other recreational facilities in the public park were also provided by the town council with a one-third funding contribution from the Miner's Welfare Committee. But the town came close to losing its institute in 1952 when a fire broke out in the basement. It was discovered by a local policeman and firemen from Lochgelly and Cowdenbeath had to tear up the floor of the games room to get at the blaze.

As demand for coal fell and the numbers of pit closures rose, the optimism that greeted nationalisation evaporated. There were many disputes and demonstrations, like this one in the early 1960s with a contingent of Lochgelly miners heading for London to protest against closures. The targets of their banner were the Prime Minister, Harold MacMillan, and NCB Chairman, Alf (later Lord) Robens. He was a former Labour MP and government minister, who managed the widespread pit-closure programme in the 1960s without provoking a major strike.

The Nelly Pit, Lochgelly

The Lochgelly Iron and Coal Company worked their Mary and Nellie pits as 'Lochgelly Colliery'. The Mary No. 1 shaft (not to be confused with the Fife Coal Company's Mary Colliery at Lochore) was sunk in 1872, but only worked for a few years. No. 2 shaft was sunk in 1886, subsequently deepened and continued in operation until the 1930s. The Nellie pit was sunk beside the Lochgelly to Ballingry road between 1878 and 1880. It was worked until 1894 and then closed. Reopening and deepening began in 1903 and it was working again by 1905. By the early 1960s the NCB regarded it as a pit with little future and it was closed in 1965 when the main production face had to be sealed off to contain an underground fire.

Collieries often lay abandoned for a long time, but only a couple of years after closure this derelict Nellie site was cleared as part of Fife Council's remarkable Lochore Meadows reclamation scheme (see pages 57 and 58). This little verse by Iain Chalmers of Cowdenbeath, neatly describes what a closed colliery site was like:

There's naethin' sae sad, forlorn, withoot hope,
As a colliery wheel, withoot ony rope.

The presence of ironstone led to industrial-scale mining being developed in the Lochgelly area much earlier than other parts of Fife. Blast furnaces were set up in 1847 but ceased operation in 1875. The Lochgelly Iron Company briefly contemplated starting them up again when they took over Blairhall pit. The end of iron working led to an expansion of the company's coal mining operations and a change of name to the Lochgelly Iron and Coal Company. Their Jenny Gray No. 1 pit was sunk to over 80 fathoms in 1854 and was subsequently augmented by another two shafts in 1889 and 1927. It was closed in 1959.

These pithead lassies are at the Jenny Gray picking tables. Although women were confined to surface jobs like picking, the male-dominated world of mining often named its pits after the wife or daughter of the pit owner. Jenny Gray was neither. Apparently, she was a smallholder whose plot of land was named after her and the pit was named after it. Another (tenuous) agricultural link occurred in 1874 when thieves, who had stolen a slaughtered pig, panicked and threw it down the shaft.

Within a few years North and South Glencraig, Crosshill and Lochore grew from nothing into large village communities. Houses were built by the Wilson's and Clyde Coal Company, who provided running water, and the Fife Coal Company who didn't. Shops showed some architectural variety. On the right of the upper picture of South Glencraig's 'Business Centre' is a branch of the Lochgelly Equitable Co-operative Society, the local version of the co-operative movement that offered affordable shopping along with a 'divi' (dividend). Typical of hastily erected mining villages are the unmade roads and feet, shod or not, simply carried dirt into the houses. In dry weather a horse-drawn water tank came round, spraying the roads to keep down the dust. Unsurprisingly, these West Fife villages became bastions of the political left – 'little Moscows'. They elected Britain's only communist MP, Willie Gallacher, and a number of communist councillors. They also nurtured prominent trade unionists like Scottish NUM President Abe Moffat, from Lumphinnans, and Lawrence Daly from Glencraig who was NUM General Secretary at the time of the national strikes of 1972 and 1974. Glencraig came to be dominated by huge bings which spread dust, dirt and sulphurous fumes. In the 1950 the old houses were cleared by Fife County Council and the people moved to Ballingry.

Fleein' doos was a miners' passion. Andrew Pratt, from Crosshill, bred, showed and raced pigeons for over fifty years and was a founder member of the Glencraig Homing Society. He worked at the Mary Colliery at Lochore.

The Fife Coal Company was responsible for much of the development of Lochore. Their Mary pit is seen here beyond the village with the Kelty collieries in the distance. Sinking of the Mary began in March 1902 to reach an estimated 30 million tons of coal. The shaft was large, nearly 30 feet by 12 feet, and at 335 fathoms, was the deepest in the country at the time. It was topped by a lattice steel headframe made by Balfour's of Leven. The winding engine, made by Douglas and Grant of Kirkcaldy, was designed to draw in one shift what Aitken Colliery did in two. It had winding rope of twice the normal strength and, in one lift, could raise eight 15 cwt. hutches on double-decked cages. The 180 foot lum had the initials FCC built into it in polychrome brick.

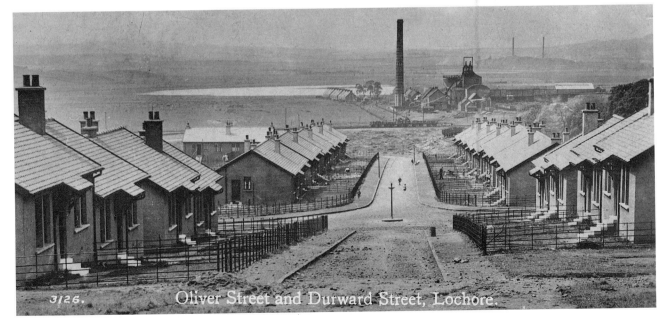

3126. Oliver Street and Durward Street, Lochore.

The Dunfermline Splint seam was reached in September 1906. Less than two years later, in February 1908 a series of explosions in the Mynheer seam killed three men and injured five. The men who died had belled for the cage after the first explosion and were waiting for it when another explosion blew them into the shaft. The other men in the pit made their way through the one and a half mile connecting tunnel to the Aitken shaft.

A second Mary shaft, with an unusual concrete headframe, was sunk in the 1920s. It helped to alleviate ventilation problems in the deeper seams. It was operated by the electric winding engine on the right. The Mary was expected to provide employment for 1,000 men for fifty years. It kept going for sixty, closing in September 1966.

Most central Fife collieries were started in the late nineteenth or early twentieth centuries, and most closed in the 1950s and 60s. For over sixty years therefore, tens of thousands of men sent tens of millions of tons of coal to the surface – and with it a vast amount of debris. When it all ended, Fife Council was left with the unwelcome legacy of a blighted landscape, subsidence and enormous bings. They reacted positively. The first reclamation scheme was the removal of a bing at Hill of Beath in 1963 which was followed by other schemes to remove bings and reclaim land flooded by subsidence. In 1966 the Council, using the experience gained through these projects, launched the biggest scheme tackled anywhere in the country – the restoration of Lochore Meadows, which, as can be seen above and right, at the time bore little resemblance to a meadow!

Bowhill bing, with the flooded Minto shaft in the foreground.

Lochore Meadows had the lot: flooded land, old railways, derelict buildings and a vast ugly bingscape. Some of the bings were burning. Beneath a brittle crust, temperatures in the Glencraig bing reached over 400°C, cool compared to Mary's 700°C, rising to 1000°C.

The scheme, covering 4 square miles and 15 million cubic yards of waste, was divided into six phases. As well as removing bings, land was drained, hollows filled, derelict buildings were demolished, and roads and foundations grubbed up. It took ten years, but when it was finished, industrial sites, agricultural land, woodlands and the award winning Lochore Meadows Country Park had been created. In the centre of the park is the loch, an area of land flooded by subsidence. Its banks were built up by colliery waste and the level fixed by a controlling weir. The mineral railway that crossed it was cut into a chain of tree-covered islands.

The once blighted landscape now hosts nature trails, children's play parks, water sports and even a beach! The Mary No. 2 concrete headframe and an old pug have been retained as reminders of the mining industry.

Mine water is another unwelcome environmental legacy. When polluted water from the flooded Minto Colliery comes to the surface it is red from oxidising iron and acidic from sulphur. To prevent contamination of the River Ore, the Government's Coal Authority has diverted the water through a 10,000 square metre reed bed which filters out the poisons before they enter the river.

The Lochgelly Iron and Coal Company began sinking Minto in 1903. It was on Brigghills farm, so it was known by that name too. This picture probably shows it during sinking with some surface buildings erected and temporary-looking headframes.

Minto had two shafts, No. 1 at 101 fathoms and No. 2 at 165 fathoms. It was a profitable operation despite having difficult roof conditions and being prone to spontaneous combustion. It latterly suffered from water problems caused by the closure of neighbouring pits. It closed in 1967. James McKelvie & Company, whose waggons are prominent in the picture, was a Dundee shipping agent.

Sinking of the Bowhill Coal Company's new colliery at Auchterderran was begun in 1895. The first working level was established at the Lochgelly Splint and Parrot Coal seam at 171 fathoms, but No. 1 shaft was deepened to the Five Feet seam at 218 fathoms after a borehole proved the lower seams. Water delayed the sinking, so the working pit was equipped with pumps which could lift 1,600 gallons a minute. The colliery was taken over by the Fife Coal Company in 1909.

The pit's worst accident occurred during a maintenance shift on the last Saturday of October, 1931. Ten men were altering the position of a fan on the east side of Hutt's Dook in the Five Feet seam when there was an explosion. They were all killed. The other men in the pit tried to reach them, but were driven back by whitedamp. The cause was never established, but the lack of ventilation, caused by the fan being out of action, allowed gas to accumulate.

In August 1952 the NCB began sinking a new No. 3 shaft. It was intended to have two working levels at 360 and 440 fathoms. At the same time, improvements in the old Nos. 1 and 2 pits included the replacement of the steam winding engines with electric ones, and the old hutches with mine cars. An underground power house and a new central washery for the pits of the Ore Valley were also built. The scheme was intended to raise output from 1,500 tons a day to 5,000, but it never reached that target. The new shaft only worked for about two years in the early 1960s and in July 1965, with output dropping and losses mounting, the pit was closed.

Bowhill Colliery, Cardenden

"Digging" Navigation Coal Seam, Bowhill Colliery, Cardenden

The coal used in ships was carefully selected. The Admiralty only bought from approved seams in approved collieries. Few met their high standards, but some Fife seams did – handy for Rosyth which would otherwise have had to import its coal from Wales! The Five Feet seam at Bowhill was a good 'Navigation Coal'. In the geological past it had been heated by volcanic action which had driven out elements like oxygen and hydrogen and enhanced the carbon content. It was therefore a hard, sulphur-free coal which burned with slight flame at high temperatures and left little ash.

Bowhill Colliery, "Brushing Road," Cardenden

The men working here in a road at Bowhill are brushers whose job was to enlarge the roads and keep them clear. To do this they had to remove rock, often with explosives, from the roof or pavement (the pit floor).

Self Acting Incline Drum, Bowhill Colliery, Cardenden

Collieries used a variety of haulage systems in the miles of roads and many levels being worked. Ponies were used in some pits, but were phased out sooner in Fife than in other areas. In big collieries with steep gradients and high output, steam engines were used. Some haulage engines were mounted on the surface and used ropes, fed down the shaft through a series of pulleys, to drive underground mechanisms. Engines set up underground were fed by steam pipes from above. Small haulage engines, like this one working an incline in the Jubilee seam at Bowhill, hauled hutches from the working areas to the main roads. From there, the main haulage engine moved them to the shaft bottom.

Bowhill Colliery, Pit Bottom, Cardenden

At the shaft bottom, the onsetters, or pit bottomers, pushed full hutches on to the cages and pulled the empty ones off. The Bowhill shafts were fitted with large cages which held four hutches on one deck.

Joe Corrie wrote plays, poems and stories, although his early upbringing was hardly geared to such a career. When he was a small boy the family moved from Slamannan to Cardenden. He was fourteen when he started work at the pits in 1908 and when his father died six years later, he became the family's breadwinner until his younger brothers were old enough to work. He was unemployed when he started writing articles for a radical miners' newspaper published after the First World War and continued to write for socialist papers during the troubled 1920s. He wrote his first play, *In Time O' Strife*, in 1926. It portrayed life for a Fife mining family during the strike of that year and the local drama group, the Bowhill Players, working professionally and renamed the Fife Miner Players, performed it to popular acclaim around the country. It was his biggest success. He later wrote a number of one act plays for performance by amateur drama groups and continued to write and publish poetry. He died in 1968.

Like football, the performing arts offered people an escape from pit life, if only for a few hours. Here the Fife Miners Band are on stage in the 1930s, 'in syncopation'! The venue is thought to be the Hippodrome at Hamilton.

Brothers Tom and Charlie Barr were miners whose family had moved from Ayrshire to Lochgelly. They perfected a strong-man act and were accepted for a summer season with Duffy's Circus in Ireland, but only if they could stage two different acts. In nine weeks they devised an acrobatic act which proved to be more popular than the weight-lifting. The following summer, after working through the winter in the Jenny Gray pit, they joined another circus, but this time the 'Barr Brothers' appeared as acrobats and comedians. They never went back to the pits. A pantomime date was followed by a summer show, and then a change of identity. They recruited an accomplice and as 'The Three Aberdonians' – "too mean to tell you what they do" – appeared for the first time at the Cinema-de-Luxe in Lochgelly. They went on to play in theatres all over Britain and became established variety artists. Moving up the bill, they appeared at the Coliseum in London and toured to Australia and Denmark where their comedy patter, delivered in Danish with a Fife accent, went down a storm. Their crowning moment came in 1938 when they appeared in a Royal Command Performance. The picture shows accomplice Rosa Louise balancing between Tom (left) and Charlie.

Band music was so popular in mining communities that, according to popular myth, boys were registered as bandsmen from the day they were born and instruments were handed down through so many generations that they ended up without a note left in them. Competitions were keenly contested and organised on divisional lines, like football leagues. Here, a band from Cardenden proudly display a trophy.

These men from the Cardenden area are displaying a trophy won for quoiting, or 'kiteing' as it was pronounced. It was a very popular sport in mining communities throughout Scotland. The heavy iron rings, seen below the cup and on the ground, were hurled 18 yards at a pin stuck in a 3 foot square bed of clay. It was a game of strength, skill and stamina and was usually played on a grassless 'green' close to a pub.

If Auchterderran, Bowhill and Cardenden were the 'ABC' of Fife's mining communities, Dundonald was the 'D'. This picture shows surface workers at Dundonald pit in 1910. The man on the right is holding a 'harp', a shovel with spaces which allowed him to leave small lumps of coal and dross behind. Some of these people may have been victims of a highway robber. In August 1920 two pay clerks, travelling to the pit in a horse-drawn governess car, were held up at gunpoint by a masked man who demanded the bag containing the wages. One of the clerks tried to grab the gun, but the barrel went up his sleeve and a shot went through his clothing and lodged in the wood of the cart. Threatened with further violence the men handed over the bag and the robber made off. Later that afternoon a miner found some of the money and the police found the revolver. By 5.00 p.m. a man had been detained in the cells at Lochgelly.

The Dundonald Coal Company's Lady Helen shaft started operating in 1892 and was taken over by the Lochgelly Iron and Coal Company about 1910. The colliery also included a mine, known as the West Mine, which worked the Little Splint seam. The houses on the right were erected in 1925. They had three apartments a bathroom, scullery and running water.

Drivage of Dundonald No. 2 surface mine was completed in 1954 and contact made with the Five Feet seam. It was being worked from the Lady Helen shaft, but No. 2 mine was developed to extend the workings. Drop-bottom mine-cars were moved underground by battery locomotives and brought to the surface by a fixed haulage engine. They were unloaded into hoppers beneath the gantry, as at Benarty (see page 39). Dundonald Colliery closed in 1964.

Just when people thought that the din and dirt of the coal industry was a thing of the past, along came opencast to extract coal not worked by deep miners. Pits and mines could have become dangerously unstable if every seam had been worked and it was also impractical to take out some seams because they were too thin or of poor quality. But with power stations able to burn a variety of blended coals, opencasters can sell all the coal they dig. Sometimes their operations expose old workings, like this roadway at Dundonald.

Sinking of Kinglassie Colliery's 180 fathom shafts was hampered by heavy inflows of water, but by about 1910 the pit was producing coal. Two drift mines were opened in the 1930s to work an area of Lochgelly Splint. They also came in handy when No. 2 shaft partly collapsed in 1960 because a connecting road from them kept the pit going until the shaft was repaired. When the Rothes Colliery at Thornton was being sunk in the 1940s and 50s, it drew the water away from Kinglassie which became hot and dry. The pit closed at the end of 1966. At one time Kinglassie had a watchman who, in his younger days, performed a strong-man act at the Links Market in Kirkcaldy. He tore packs of cards, bent pokers and began the act by carrying a pony on to the stage – so who needs video security when the watchman lifts horses for a hobby!

When the NCB took over the industry they looked at the possibility of sinking a new colliery to extract reserves from an isolated basin at Westfield, a mile to the west of Kinglassie. By the mid-1950s they had changed their minds and announced plans to work the site by opencast. It started in 1960 and produced about 20,000 tons a week – 40% of Scotland's opencast output. It became the biggest opencast site in Britain, the biggest in Europe

for bituminous coal, and Europe's biggest hole. By the time the 'Big Hole' was exhausted in the mid-1980s, it was 900 feet deep and 1.5 miles in diameter. The NCB even had to construct a new Kinninmont Farm when the hole got too close to the existing steading. The Lurgi pressure-gasification plant can be seen in the distance.

The Lurgi plant, opened in 1960, made gas from coal cheaper than any other process could. It used low rank coals from the Westfield site which the NCB originally thought would have to be discarded, in effect creating a new source of fuel. The plant produced gas at very high pressure and when it was opened, it provided the base load for central Scotland's gas supply. The Queen officially opened the plant on a dry, windy day in 1961. As part of the ceremonial proceedings the Duke of Edinburgh used a digger to load coal into a tipper truck at Westfield, which helped to make it the dustiest, dirtiest and smelliest royal visit ever.

The Star Coal Company worked a small basin of coal near the hamlet of Star in the 1920s. The ramshackle-looking mine employed only a handful of men. The six here are, from left to right, William Annandale, William Paton, James Gourlay, Alex Wishart, John Grierson and Thomas Rutherford. Little mines that worked isolated pockets of coal were a useful source of employment and fuel for local communities. But the local community had reason to curse the little mine when it was pumped clear of water and drained the village supply as well.

Mine openings, like this entrance to the Star Mine, were known by Scottish miners as 'in-gaun een' – in-going eyes.

The Cornish beam pumping engine kept mines free of water and allowed deeper mines to be sunk. It was a huge advance in mining technology and engine-houses like this were once a common sight. This one is at Middlefield, beside the new Glenrothes With Thornton station. Fife has three such buildings remaining: this one, one on Preston Island and another at Kilmux near Leven.

Thornton Mine was another of the Fife Coal Company's post-war drift mines. It was still being developed when the NCB took it over. Like Benarty, it was operated with drop-bottom mine cars which were unloaded into hoppers ready for onward transport by road. It was a short-lived operation, closing in 1953.

Rothes Colliery was started by the Fife Coal Company but became a 'flagship project' for the NCB. The first sod was cut by C. Augustus Carlow, chairman of the company in December 1946. He used a silver spade which had been presented to his mother when she inaugurated the Mary Pit at Lochore in 1902. Work on the actual sinking of No. 1 shaft began in August 1948 and about a year later No. 2 shaft was begun. They soon hit water-bearing sandstone. Water poured out at a rate of about 100 gallons a minute and only the skill and experience of the contractors, the Cementation Company, kept the shafts moving downwards. By the end of 1950, when this picture of the sinking headframes was taken, the two shafts were about 100 fathoms deep and months behind schedule. An epic battle between man and the elements was developing.

Rothes was to be worked by 'horizon mining', a technique in which access mines are driven from the shaft across the strata to act as level roads for locomotives and mine cars. At Rothes, the seams dipped steeply before levelling out and becoming thick. To gain access to this bonanza the shafts were to be sunk to 470 fathoms and horizons opened up at this and higher levels. Through 1951 the sinkers made reasonable progress, but in 1952 more water shot into the shaft under pressure. Progress was painfully slow. Sinking of No. 2 shaft was stopped in 1953 at 275 fathoms and work, seen here, was begun on opening out the 266 fathom horizon. No. 1 shaft encountered more water-bearing sandstone in 1954 and in early February 1955 it hit whinstone. Whin is normally hard and stable, but this was fissured and water poured out of it. Despite the frustrations, Cementation pushed on and reached 418 fathoms in February 1956, seven and half years after sinking began.

Above ground, the pithead buildings went up around the sinking headframes, but this was no ordinary colliery. Instead of the old jumble of structures, a new style of colliery complex was created by the NCB's Scottish Division architect, Egon Riss, an Austrian wartime refugee. He designed elegant concrete winding towers and a unified set of buildings that allowed the miners to be under cover from the moment they arrived at work to when they left after their shower at the end of a shift.

Faces in the Five Feet seam were opened out on the 266 fathom horizon and the first coal came to the surface in June 1957. Within a year the Lochgelly Splint seam was also being worked. The Queen visited the pit on 30th June 1958, but there was anxiety beneath the smiles. Mining conditions were proving difficult. The Five Feet seam was less than two feet thick and had been burned by volcanic rock, while the roof was bad and the area faulted. Of sixteen faces opened out, fourteen were abandoned and output never got beyond 40% of its target. The 266 fathom level was always likely to be the least productive in the colliery, but its poor performance blighted the pit. Underground mines dipping to 333 fathoms were started, but in March 1962 work on the project was stopped. The colliery had been expected to cost £1.65 million and produce 5,000 tons a day for 100 years, but when development ceased it had cost over £20 million and produced only a fraction of its intended output.

The winding towers were demolished in March 1993, but some surface buildings and the fan évasés remain as a reminder that in mining, nothing is guaranteed.

Rothes was an important element of the NCB's drive to open up new coalfields, but it was in Fife and the experienced miners were in Lanarkshire. To accommodate them the new town of Glenrothes was begun. It had well-appointed houses which were a vast improvement on the run-down rows of the west and yet people were reluctant to move. They feared losing familiar things – friends, neighbours, the pub, club and football team. They also feared criticism from local people for jumping the housing queue. But jobs in the old 'black country' were dying and slowly migration got under way, not just to Glenrothes, but to the Lothians, Ayrshire and other parts of Fife as well. As it gathered pace the NCB believed it was engaged in one the biggest movements of people in Scotland's history. But old habits died hard and some wives from the old rows were unhappy that Glenrothes delivery vans stopped at the end of a path instead of at the front door as they were used to.

Efforts were made to ensure that Glenrothes had a mixed industrial base and was not a one-industry town. The Motherwell mining equipment manufacturer Anderson Boyes was one company which opened a factory in the new town. Nevertheless, the loss of Rothes pit was a severe blow which the new town's Development Corporation met head-on by planning for growth. Former miners were retrained, new industries were brought in and the population target raised. The new town is now a thriving well-established centre.

East Fife's second major new sinking after the Second World War was at Seafield, south of Kirkcaldy. Mrs W.H. Craig, wife of the NCB's Divisional Marketing Director, cut the first sod on 12th May 1954. She is seen here flanked by East Fife Area General Manager, Mr F.M.T. Bunney, and the Rev. J.A. Sim who dedicated the project. Alongside are the area's two youngest employees, trainees Cameron Stewart from Wellesley Colliery (with the wheelbarrow) and James Hodges from Michael Colliery. When the ceremony was over, the sinking crew, clad in white coats (I wonder how long they stayed white?), swung the first kibble into place and filled it while the Michael Colliery pipe band played 'Heilan Laddie'.

The new colliery was intended to work reserves under the Forth which extended from Fife to the Lothians, although not even Coal Board optimists expected the pit to link up with Prestongrange or Monktonhall. Two 24 foot diameter shafts were sunk to 317 fathoms and two working levels established at 166 and 308 fathoms. No. 1 shaft was for winding coal in skips, while No. 2 was for men, materials and stone. These separate functions meant that the winding towers were of different heights, giving the colliery a distinctive architectural appearance. Mine workings under water had to be a set distance below the rock cover. So, while the shafts were being sunk, five small boats conducted a seismic survey of the sea bed to discover how much mud and sand covered the rock.

The Seafield seams dipped steeply, as demonstrated by this man-riding vehicle. The gradient contributed to a tragic accident in May 1973 when men were moving the face-line supports forward after the shearer had made its cut. Before the supports could be pressurised, the roof collapsed, knocking them over like dominoes. Five men were killed and four injured. The accident happened in the Dysart Main seam which sloped at 1 in 1.52, a gradient described officially as "extremely severe".

After nationalisation the work of the Miners' Welfare Fund was split. Social welfare became the responsibility of a new body called the Coal Industry Social Welfare Organisation (CISWO) and industrial welfare came under the NCB. They took health and safety at work very seriously and made significant improvements. They appointed medical officers at Divisional and Area level and built medical centres at large collieries like this one at Seafield. The centres also served the smaller collieries in an area. They were staffed by State Registered Nurses, assisted by trained first-aiders.

Seafield was expected to maintain an output of 5,000 tons of coal a day for sixty years. After that it was anticipated that new mines could be developed which would extend the pit's life to 150 years. Production began in 1960 and by the end of the decade the pit was living up to all of the NCB's optimistic predictions. It broke production records week after week and was the first pit in Scotland to produce more than 30,000 tons a week. It exceeded that in July 1970 when figures of 67.8 cwt. per man-shift and up to 7,600 tons per 24 hours helped to achieve a week's output of over 36,000 tons. But that was the high point and by early 1984 it was said to be one of Britain's highest loss-making pits. It closed in 1988.

Tucked in on the shore behind Dysart's Pan Ha' was the Lady Blanche pit. It worked a system of mining known as 'stoop and room' in which large pillars of coal (stoops) are left to support the roof while the coal is extracted around them, leaving empty space (rooms). In 1914 'hydraulic stowage' was used in an attempt to take out the stoops. A mixture of sand, crushed waste and water was pumped into the 'rooms' where it set hard and by supporting the roof in this way it was hoped to win 100,000 tons of coal. Lady Blanche was closed in 1928, but retained as a ventilation shaft for the Frances Colliery to which it was connected underground.

The Lady Blanche and Frances pits belonged to the Earl of Rosslyn's Collieries Ltd which was taken over by the Fife Coal Company in 1923. The Frances shaft (it was originally 'Francis' – the male spelling) went into production in 1878 to work reserves which were mainly under the sea. It was sunk to 100 fathoms on a narrow strip of ground above sea cliffs known as the Dubbie Braes – the pit was also known as the 'Dubbie'. (Dub is the Scots word for pond, puddle or pool – also a sea pool from which the Braes no doubt took their name). Frances lived up to the name too and water, either alkaline or acidic depending on the level it was coming from, was pumped out at the rate of 1,600 gallons a minute.

The Fife Coal Company installed a new washery in this building in 1925. It could deal with 100 tons of small sized coal an hour, the larger lumps being separated on the picking tables. The washery also handled output from the colliery's surface mine which worked coal to the landward side of the shaft and in the NCB days it took coal from Thornton Mine. To begin with the NCB used the Frances washer for small-sized coal and sent larger lumps to the Bowhill treatment plant, but the old plant became disused when coal from the Frances was sent to the large capacity preparation plant at Seafield.

The Fife Coal Company started redeveloping the pit in the late 1930s, although the work was interrupted by the Second World War and completed by the NCB. Site restrictions dictated that the winder should be placed at one end of the elliptical shaft and the new headframe fitted with pulley wheels mounted in tandem instead of side by side. The upper wheel and its cage were known as Dysart (because they were on that side of the shaft) and the lower one Wemyss.

As part of the redevelopment the workings were extended on the seaward side of a thick whinstone dyke that cut across the coal measures. When the drivage broke through the dyke it struck coal, but no one knew which seam. Experts were called in, but they too were baffled. One suggested that his wife, a palynologist (a geologist who specialises in fossil-spores), should be consulted. The higher echelons of the Fife Coal Company were appalled at the idea of a woman – 'a housewife' – coming to the aid of the macho world of mining, but General Manager Charles Reid agreed. Dr (Mrs) Knox collected samples from the adjacent collieries and by analysing them discovered that the dyke had acted like a fault and pushed the coal-bearing strata up to a higher level on the landward side. Her findings were proved by a rising bore. The redevelopment, which included the introduction of locomotive haulage and large capacity mine cars, was completed in 1957 and daily output raised from 1,100 to 1,800 tons.

Frances had access to vast undersea coal reserves, but during the 1984 strike fires caused by spontaneous combustion broke out and the colliery was shut down, although not closed entirely. It was kept on a care and maintenance basis and for a number of years a small group of men – this electrician at the Sandwell Dook haulage engine was one of them – kept the pumps and other equipment going. Plans were drawn up for what would have been in effect an entirely new colliery with dipping mines running to the base of the undersea coal measures. It would have been Scotland's ultimate super mine extending all the way to the Lothians, but would have needed costly, extended haulage systems and so it remained a plan. The pithead buildings were demolished leaving the headframe standing as a gaunt reminder of Fife's mining past.

The third of the Earl of Rosslyn's pits was the Randolph Colliery beside the Kirkcaldy to Windygates road. It was opened about 1850, although some of the workings were even older and extended as far as Thornton. It had two shafts, No. 1 to 63 fathoms and No. 2 to 83 fathoms. It worked the Lower Dysart seam which had two layers of coal separated by a band of stone and so a lot of debris went up the shaft to enlarge the bing. The Randolph was noted for being a safety conscious 'happy pit', with strike-free working relations that owed a lot to a consultative committee and the manager, J.S. Saunders. He was the first colliery manager in Scotland to be awarded an MBE for his services to the industry. Randolph was also a wet pit with 2,000 gallons of acidic and highly corrosive water being pumped to the surface every minute. The pit closed in 1968.

Wemyss Collieries' No. 7 pit was sunk on the sea shore beside West Wemyss harbour. It had been working for a few years before it was named Victoria in honour of the Queen's coronation in 1837. It was notable for having what could have been the earliest pithead baths in Scotland – wooden tubs supplied with boiler water. Being next to the harbour the pit was well placed for exports, with rails able to take hutches of coal virtually from pit to ship. The last coal shipment from the harbour was in 1915, after which Victoria's coal was brought to the surface at other linked shafts. When the Victoria closed it was used as a ventilation shaft for Lochhead Colliery.

The King Decorates Brave Heroes,
at Buckingham Palace, July

Mr. Geo. Dryburgh and Mr. James Dryburgh,
Who went down a Burning Pit in Wemyss Collieries, Fifeshire,
to try to rescue fellow-workmen.

When John Kilpatrick didn't return from inspecting the Victoria on 29th December 1907, engineman David Black became alarmed. Two men, Andrew Morris, and William Scott, went down to see what was wrong. They also failed to return and the engineman sent for assistance. George and James Dryborough volunteered to investigate. They were nearly overcome by gas and only had time to drag Morris' body on to the cage before signalling to return. The gas was coming from an old fire that had reignited. It could have been worse – it happened on a Sunday; on a weekday 250 men would have been at risk. Risking their lives, engineman Black and another man, Alexander Walker, went down and recovered William Scott's body. Walker rushed fifty yards in an attempt to find Kilpatrick, but had to turn back. The Dryboroughs were honoured for their part in the rescue attempt and recalled that when they visited London to receive their medals, they were photographed by ". . . they boxes for taking our faces . . .". This postcard was made from one of the pictures.

Lochhead Colliery was originally called the Lady Lilian. It was sunk in the 1890s on the site of old workings and linked underground to Victoria Colliery. When West Wemyss harbour stopped shipping coal, the process was reversed and Victoria's output came up at Lochhead. The Dysart Main seam at Lochhead was 23 feet thick and prone to spontaneous combustion – mining altered geological pressures and exposed coal to oxygen – a potentially lethal combination. If a thick seam was to be extracted safely and successfully, the roof had to remain unbroken and all the coal taken out. It was removed in layers, or lifts, and for a while hydraulic stowage was used to support the roof, as at Lady Blanche. This was stopped after the 1926 strike and the seam lay fallow until 1938 when 'pneumatic stowage' was introduced. This used a mixture of washer refuse, crushed table pickings and boiler ash blown into the workings to form a solid mass. Nevertheless, 'heating' remained a serious problem and by the time Lochhead closed in 1970 hundreds of stoppings (barriers) had been built to contain fires.

These people have been using a Lochhead hutch to gather funds at a gala in aid of the Randolph Wemyss Memorial Hospital. They won first prize too! The pony is wearing eye protectors from the pit. People's clothes and the soldier's uniform would suggest a date around the First World War, but the miner's carbide lamp is of little help in dating the picture as lamps like this were in use for about fifty years after their introduction in 1905. They had two reservoirs, one for water and the other for calcium carbide, and when these were mixed they made a gas, ethyne or acetylene, which burned with a bright flame.

Above: Old Scottish villages associated with mining were known as 'coal towns'. Most that survive and retain such names are in Fife – Coaltown of Wemyss is one. It was originally two hamlets, Easter and Wester Coaltown, which became one as the industry developed. When Lochhead pit was opened, Coaltown was rebuilt as a new 'model' village. It was designed by Alexander Tod, who was responsible for Wemyss estate developments at the time. As well as housing, the village had shops, a school and a school of needlework. The Earl David, a Gothenburg-style pub, was opened in 1911 and the miners' institute, in the centre of this picture, opened in 1925.

The Wemyss Coal Company began opening the Earlseat mines into the Dysart Main seam in 1904. The five drift mines radiated from a central treatment point which was connected to the company railway by a two and a half mile branch line. Men travelled to the mines on a special train known (with some cynicism) as the 'Garden City Express' or 'Whippet' because it was often held up by mineral traffic. In August 1907 it was waiting for a coal train to clear the line when that train's driver lost control. Men leapt to safety seconds before the old carriages were smashed to pieces. The mines were abandoned after the 1926 strike. The NCB opened the mine in the lower picture at Earlseat in 1951, and closed it at the end of 1958 to reduce overall capacity – even though it was producing 88,000 tons a year, at a notional profit!

The sinking of the Michael Colliery at East Wemyss was begun shortly after the formation of the Wemyss Coal Company in 1894. Initially there were two rectangular shafts, 12 yards apart, sunk to the Chemiss seam at 136 fathoms. The pit produced its first coal in 1898 and output settled at around 1,000 tons a day. Like the other coastal collieries, the Michael's 'take' was from seams that dipped steeply under the sea.

In the late 1920s the company decided to deepen the workings, but instead of extending the existing arrangements they took the bold option of sinking a new No. 3 shaft. It was 160 yards from the old ones, circular, concrete-lined and sunk to the Lower Dysart seam at 300 fathoms. It was begun in 1928 and brought its first coal to the surface in 1931. The steel headframe was topped with 20 foot diameter pulley wheels, and a 50 foot high gantry was erected to take the hutches from the new shaft to a rebuilt screening plant. Redevelopment of No. 2 started in 1935. The original square shaft was enlarged as a circular shaft, deepened with a circular extension to the Bowhouse seam and connected to the Dysart Main by an underground mine. When the work was completed at the end of 1936, the company had in effect created a new colliery on the same site. It was set to become Scotland's No. 1. The picture shows the No. 3 headgear with Methil, Largo Law and the East Neuk Coast in the background.

Blacksmiths, like this group at the Michael Colliery, were essential to any pit. In the early days they sharpened miners' picks and fitted shoes on the ponies. Although these chores disappeared, blacksmiths continued to connect cages to winding ropes with chains and capels, and make and repair items of equipment.

The Michael was the best producing pit inherited by the NCB in Scotland, but output slumped during a redevelopment that began in 1949 and finished in 1963. It included deepening No. 2 shaft and replacing haulage systems with locomotives. The previous owners, the Wemyss Coal Company, had expected a similar scheme to take eight years. The pit was beginning to recover by 1967, but at about 3.30 a.m. on 9th September fire was discovered. It was well alight when the alarm was raised twenty minutes later. The delay was caused by uncertainty as the

temperature change, noxious emissions and smell of a fire had been masked by polyurethane foam which had been used to line the area. When the flames broke through, they ignited the foam and spread to the conveyor belt, coal and wood. The dense and irritating smoke got into the intake airways, and quickly affected every area of the pit. Three hundred and two men got out, but nine didn't make it. The fire was sealed off and the colliery closed.

The enquiry into the incident recommended that polyurethane foam should not be used in a coal mine again – with the benefit of hindsight it seems incredible that it ever was! The pit was kept on a care and maintenance basis for a while, but never reopened. There was one positive outcome as self-rescuers, breathing devices which had been introduced at some collieries on an experimental basis, were adopted universally. They gave men about thirty minutes to get clear of the kind of smoke and fumes experienced in the Michael fire. The picture from 1954 shows rescue men at the pit in happier times.

These stylish colliery offices at the Michael were adjacent to No. 3 shaft – the walkway leading from them gave access to the shaft. Most of East Wemyss was in close proximity to the pit. As with all mining communities attended by disaster, it was devastated by the fire and subsequent pit closure. A memorial, with a mini-replica of No. 3 headframe, has been erected in the village.

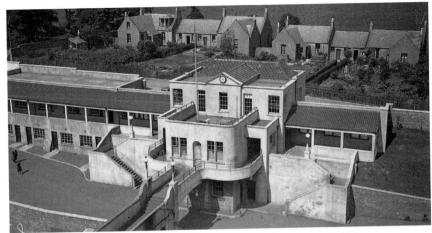

These Wemyss Coal Company offices were where the company's agents, accountants, surveyors and other staff were based.

This postcard was sent from the offices to a mining engineer on holiday in Perthshire in 1909. It is clearly unofficial although the drawings are interesting and include a tally lamp, pithead frame and surveyor's dial. This was like a large compass and used to plot locations underground.

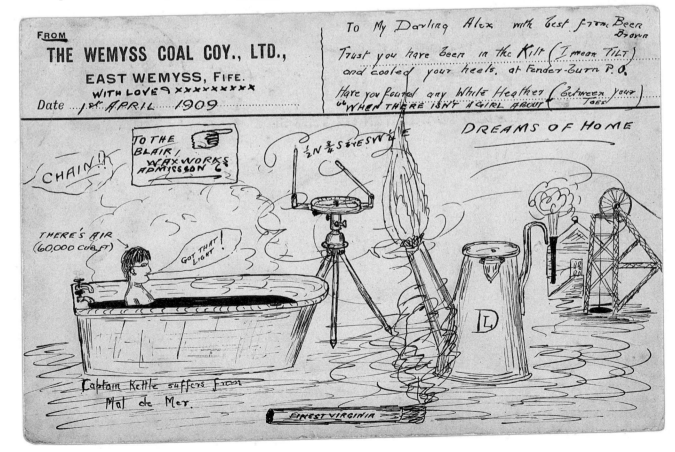

Sailing is not normally associated with mining communities, but along the East Fife coast from Kirkcaldy to Methil many miners kept square-rigged yawls. Some men built their own. They used them for fishing and raced them in regattas, like this one at West Wemyss. These regattas were like galas to the East Fife villages. In the background are the chimney and bing of the Rosie pit.

Rosie village outside East Wemyss was built for miners, and their families, employed at Bowman and Company's Rosie pit. The two shafts were 100 fathoms deep and 10 yards apart. No. 1 was started in 1879 and took eighteen months to sink while No. 2 was begun in 1881 and finished in a year. The winding engine drum at No. 2 shaft was made so that the cages could operate to two levels. One side of the drum was 10 foot in diameter and it worked the Chemiss seam at 100 fathoms. The other side of the drum, which worked the Eight Feet seam at 60 fathoms, was 6 foot in diameter. The pit was taken over in 1905 by the Wemyss Coal Company and closed by the NCB in December 1953. The Wemyss Tramway operated between 1906 and 1932, running between Leven and Kirkcaldy and passing most of the Wemyss Coal Company pits. The company even owned its own large trams for carrying miners to and from work.

Wellsgreen Colliery, to the north of East Wemyss, was opened in the 1880s by the Fife Coal Company. It had two shafts, 45 feet apart, sunk 84 fathoms to the Dysart Main. The seam had two layers of good coal separated by a stone band. The lower coal was taken out first, followed by the upper coal. It was worked in small areas so that the ventilating current could be shut off in the event of spontaneous combustion. In later years other seams were worked, but the colliery's fortunes fluctuated. It was closed for a year in the late 1920s as part of a scheme to allow prices to recover by restricting output. An associated drift mine was opened in 1946 which fed coal directly by conveyor to the pit's screens and washer. The pit outlasted the mine by about a year, closing in April 1959.

Cameron Mine, to the west of Buckhaven, was opened in the mid-1930s by the Wemyss Coal Company. It was on the site of the old Isabella pit and had two 1,000 yard tunnels, dipping at 1 in 6 to the Bowhouse seam. The coal was loaded on to a conveyor at the face and taken to the surface. There it dropped on to another conveyor which took it to railway waggons. Closure was announced in December 1958 and with tragic irony three men were killed by a roof fall the following day. The mine closed in July 1959.

The Wemyss Coal Company centralised its coal washing and preparation at Denbeath in a 'Baum' washer which washed coal before it was sized. The process was invented by Fritz Baum, a German maker of coal-cleaning equipment. As the coal passed through wash boxes, the water was pulsated by compressed air to remove dirt and stone. The idea worked best when treating large quantities of coal, so it was ideal for a large central plant like Denbeath. It was built in 1905, only four years after Baum's experimental plant, making it one of the first in Britain. The 100 foot high structure loomed over the village of Links of Buckhaven which stood in the way of the expanding colliery and its associated railway sidings. People were moved out of their houses and the coast road to Leven was rerouted. The site was buried under tons of pit waste and another name was added to the list of Scotland's 'lost villages'.

Bowman and Company sank their Denbeath Colliery shaft between 1883 and 1885 on the site of workings developed in the seventeenth century by David, second Earl of Wemyss. The pit worked the Eight Feet seam at 115 fathoms and the Chemiss seam at 150 fathoms. The double-decked cage could take four 8 cwt. tubs and the output was 600 tons a day. When the Wemyss Coal Company took the colliery over in 1905, they sank a new elliptical shaft alongside Bowman's original and enlarged and deepened the old shaft to the Dysart Main at 264 fathoms. They more than doubled the capacity of the Baum washer and changed the colliery's name to Wellesley.

The redeveloped Wellesley Colliery went into production in 1910. The old shaft was used for man-winding while the new one mainly wound coal. Each cage could carry eight loaded hutches, making a combined weight of cage, chains, rope, hutches and coal of about 22 tons. It could be lifted to the surface in 41 seconds – an average speed of 30 m.p.h., although speeds in excess of 50 m.p.h. were also known. The steam winding engines for both shafts were made by Douglas and Grant of Kirkcaldy. Here, a train is being hauled through the colliery by an ex-Army 'Austerity' pug.

This cheery group is believed to have been photographed in front of Leven Nos. 1 and 2 pits. They were developed in 1877/78 by the Fife Coal Company on the Methil side of the River Leven. The shafts were sunk 50 feet apart to the Chemiss seam at 150 fathoms.

Underground mines running across the dipping seams opened up the Barncraig and Coxtool seams and the pit's initial production reached 800 tons a day. It was wet and the pumping engine, made by Douglas and Grant of Kirkcaldy, had to deal with 13 tons of water for every ton of coal raised. By the late 1920s severe faulting had pushed output down to 300 tons a day and although No. 1 shaft was deepened by 23 fathoms in 1929 (about the time this picture was probably taken), the pit closed in 1931.

Coal was worked in the vicinity of Methilhill in the seventeenth century, but it remained a small village until the sinking of Pirnie Colliery in the 1860s. The shafts were 400 yards apart and the pit produced 300 tons a day from narrow seams. The lease was taken over by the Fife Coal Company in 1877 and the pit was linked to Leven No. 4 pit when it was opened before the First World War. The two operations ceased in the 1920s. The development of Methilhill as a housing estate more or less coincided with the demise of the pits. The Wemyss Coal Company built 230 of these houses in 1924-25. They were a significant improvement on Denbeath houses with three or four rooms, kitchen, scullery and bathroom. More housing was added later by the County Council.

Methil Power Station was built in the 1960s to burn slurry, the sludge left after the coal washing process. It was as if the industry had turned completely on its head. At one time only the largest lumps of coal could be profitably sold, but now the electricity generators – coal's biggest market – wanted the finest particles. The slurry is beaten to a fine powder and blown into the furnace where it burns at high temperatures to produce steam to drive the turbines. Even during reclamation schemes like Lochore Meadows, tons of sludge at the bottom of old settling ponds were removed and sent to Methil to be turned into electricity.

MINERS' CONVALESCENT HOME CARLOW MEMORIAL – LEVEN

Linnwood Hall, Leven, was built in 1904 and stood in 14 acres of garden grounds. It was the former home of the Chairman of the Fife Coal Company who donated it in November 1946 for use as a convalescent home by miners' wives and female colliery workers. It was the last such gesture made by the company before nationalisation. It was officially opened in February 1948 as the C. Augustus Carlow Convalescent Home, although it was unofficially known as 'Carlow's Mansion'. It provided accommodation for thirty women. The first matron, Mrs M. Nicole Davis, had held similar posts in Scotland and also ran her own nursing home on Jersey which she left only days before the island was invaded by the German army. The home closed when its functions were transferred to the Carlow Home at Blair Castle about 1970.

The preserved windmill and salt pans at St Monance are testimony to the existence of old coal workings north and east of Leven. In 1935 a Markinch firm looked into the possibility of starting mining again at St Monance and in the 1890s attempts were made to revive Pittenweem's mines. At Billow Ness, south of Anstruther, outcrop coal was dug just after the Second World War and the NCB caused consternation in 1953 with plans to opencast a number of sites between Largo and Anstruther. Inland, there were coal workings over many years in the Largoward area including this Largoward, or Largobeath, Colliery. It was operated by the East of Fife Coal Company and worked seams of Jewel and Splint coal – the Splint was about 2 foot 6 inches thick and found at about 14 fathoms. The pit was abandoned in 1914.

This little pit is thought to be Rameldry. It operated from the early 1890s (when these pictures were probably taken) to the 1920s. It was owned by James Martin of Cults and never employed large numbers of men – the entire workforce is probably shown in the picture. It was in a small isolated coalfield close to Kingskettle and was the last working pit of any size in the area. Perhaps the most obvious indication that coal was once mined around here is the name of the village, Coaltown of Burnturk. Burnturk Colliery was the centre of a lime burning industry around 1800. Limestone was brought from quarries to the kilns along a 2 mile canal and the burnt lime, and coal, was sent to Kingskettle by another canal half a mile long. In order to keep the lumps of coal and lime unbroken, the boats on the shorter canal were quite small and propelled by a boatman hauling on a series of wooden poles suspended above the water. These Burnturk Canals were the only industrial canals of any consequence in Fife, but were disused by about 1830. Mining of limestone at Cults continued long after coal working ceased.

ACKNOWLEDGEMENTS

I am indebted to a number of people who have helped in the compilation of this book by supplying pictures and information. I would like to thank Iain Chalmers, Stuart Mathewson, Jim Hutcheson, Eileen Watt, Frank Gibb, Andrew Watson, Bernard D. Rodger, James Sommerville, Alan Brotchie, Eric Eunson, Bill Fiet, George Gillespie, Campbell Drysdale, George Archibald, Willie Brown, Terry Harrison, Margaret Graham, Margeorie Mekie and Stuart Marshall. I would also like to thank Roberta Mason of the Carlow Home for introducing me to Alex McKay, Davie Adams, Robert Raeburn, Archie Mill, Andrew Cunningham, John Fairfoul and John Docherty who all helped with some important detail.

THE PUBLISHERS REGRET THAT THEY CANNOT SUPPLY COPIES OF ANY PICTURES FEATURED IN THIS BOOK.

The following photographs are reproduced courtesy of:

(u – upper picture; m – middle picture; l – lower picture)

Scottish Mining Museum: Front Cover; 2(u&l); 3(u&l); 5; 6(l); 7(u&l); 8(u&l); 9(u&l); 11(u&l); 12(l); 14(u&l); 19(u&l); 20(u&l – left & right); 26; 27(l); 30(u&l); 31(u); 33(l); 32(u); 39(u, m&l); 41(l); 42(u&l); 43(u&l); 45(l); 46/47; 48(u); 49(l); 51(u&l); 56(l – left & right); 59(l); 67(u&l); 69(u); 71(l); 75(u&l); 76(u); 78(u&l); 79(u&l); 80/81; 84(u&l); 85(l); 89(u&l); 91(u&l); 92(u&l); 95(l); 97(u&l); 101(u); 102/103; 109(u); back cover(u).
Fife Council Planning Services: 50(l); 57(u, m&l); 58(u); 68(u); 76(l); 82(l).
Fife Council Archives: 74; 77(u, m&l).
Crown Copyright; Royal Commission on the Ancient and Historic Monuments of Scotland: 71(u). Scottish Gas Board Collection held in RCAHMS: 45(u).
Dunfermline Central Library – Local History Collection: 15(u&l); 18(l); 21(l); 22; 32(l); 35(u); 38(m).
Fife Council Libraries – Central Area, Kirkcaldy: 66(u&l).
Coal Industry Social Welfare Organisation: 55(u); 94(l).
Alan Brotchie collection: 1(u); 16/17; 18(u); 21(u); 24(l); 25(u); 27(u); 56(u); 68(l); 86(u); 87(u); 90; 93(u); 98(l); 99(u); 101(l); 104(u); 105(u); 106/107.
Eric Eunson collection: 29; 83; 87(l); 88(u&m); 93(l); 94(u); 95(u); 96(u&l); 98(u); 99(l); 100(u); 106(l); 110(l).
Scottish Power, Methil Power Station: 109(l).
Terry Harrison collection: 112.

A few anonymously published pictures appear in this book; the publishers will be pleased to entertain acknowledgements for these in future editions.

SCOTTISH MINING MUSEUM

This book would not have been possible without the help of the Scottish Mining Museum at the Lady Victoria Colliery, Newtongrange. It is ten miles south of Edinburgh on the A7 road. Visitors can tour the colliery buildings, see mining equipment at a mock-up face and visit the massive winding engine. Audio visual presentations, permanent and changing exhibitions present a history of mining life.

For opening times and further information contact:

The Scottish Mining Museum,
Lady Victoria Colliery,
Newtongrange,
Midlothian, EH22 4QN.
Telephone 0131 663 7519
Fax 0131 654 1618

Working a shortwall cutter in the Dysart Main.